C. G. Jung's Archetype Concept

I0130662

The concept of archetypes is at the core of C. G. Jung's analytical psychology. In this interesting and accessible volume, Roesler summarises the classical theory of archetypes and the archetypal stages of the individuation process as it was developed by Jung and his students. Various applications of archetypes, in cultural studies as well as in clinical practice, are demonstrated with detailed case studies, dream series, myths, fairy tales, and so on.

The book also explores how the concept has further developed as a result of research and, for the first time, integrates findings from anthropology, human genetics, and the neurosciences. Based on these contemporary insights, Roesler also makes a compelling argument for why some of Jung's views on the concept should be comprehensively revised.

Offering new insights on foundational Jungian topics like the collective unconscious, persona, and shadow, *C. G. Jung's Archetype Concept* is of great interest to Jungian students, analysts, psychotherapists, and scholars.

Christian Roesler is a professor of Clinical Psychology at the Catholic University of Applied Sciences in Freiburg, Germany, and Lecturer of Analytical Psychology at the University of Basel, Switzerland. He is also a Jungian psychoanalyst in private practice in Freiburg and a member of the faculty of the C. G. Jung-Institutes in Stuttgart and Zurich.

C. G. Jung's Archetype Concept

Theory, Research and Applications

Christian Roesler

Translated by Alexander Ulyet and Christian Roesler

Routledge
Taylor & Francis Group

LONDON AND NEW YORK

First published in English 2022
by Routledge
2 Park Square, Milton Park, Abingdon, Oxon OX14 4RN

and by Routledge
605 Third Avenue, New York, NY 10158

Routledge is an imprint of the Taylor & Francis Group, an informa business

© 2022 Christian Roesler

Translated by Alexander Ulyet and Christian Roesler

First published in German by W. Kohlhammer Verlag GmbH, 2016

British Library Cataloguing-in-Publication Data
A catalogue record for this book is available from the British Library

Library of Congress Cataloging-in-Publication Data
A catalog record has been requested for this book

ISBN: 978-0-367-52805-8 (hbk)
ISBN: 978-0-367-51053-4 (pbk)
ISBN: 978-1-003-05845-8 (ebk)

DOI: 10.4324/9781003058458

Typeset in Times New Roman
by Newgen Publishing UK

Contents

Illustrations

Figures

Table

1 Introduction

By way of an introduction to the theme of archetypes, I would like to begin with the following case study, which occurred some years ago in my practice. At the time I was giving psychotherapy to a young man in his early 20s, who had contacted me primarily because of a recurring depression. It emerged after some time and a reluctant disclosure on his part, that along with this depression came a misuse of cannabis. This abuse had gone so far that my client would often spend long periods of the day dozing. He exhibited signs of cognitive disturbances, such as difficulty in concentrating and weakness of memory, which in conjunction with his depression was causing his career to suffer. At seven years old my client had experienced the death of his mother, who had died from blood poisoning as a result of hospital treatment. From then on, he lived together with his father and his much older sister, who took over the maternal role for him in the time that she lived at home. When my client was 14 years old, his father was diagnosed with cancer and it quickly became clear that he would also die of the illness. At this time the client's older sister had already left home and lived with her partner and her own family, some distance from my client's residence. My client now had to cope, as a youth, with the slow decline and eventual death of his father and eventually remain completely alone in the now empty home of his parents. The relevant child protection services had decided that he was in a position to manage his daily life alone. My client lived alone in his parental home, cut short his schooling and

DOI: 10.4324/9781003058458-1

vocational education, and had been working, at the time that he came to me, for some years as a tradesman. He had left the family home, in which he continued to live, practically the same as how his parents had arranged it. I could not help but think at times that the whole thing seemed more like a mausoleum in which the lost parents could be remembered and less like a place to actually live.

My client's depression continued to return in episodes, particularly strongly in the time just before the anniversary of his mother's death. It was obvious that the client had been confronted with these losses far too early in his life and that he had, considering his austere living situation, in no way psychologically come to terms with them. The experience of losing his emotional foundation, of being alone, and the excessive demand of this were surely once more intensified by the premature death of his father. Psychodynamically, the genetic background for his depression can surely be found in these early losses. The excessive abuse of cannabis, with which he would shift himself into a kind of trance-like state, stood for me in this context to be an attempt to recreate a certain closeness to his lost parents. On the conscious level my client rationalised the drug abuse as a libertarian lifestyle choice and emphasised that, even as a youth, he had really appreciated being able to do what he wanted to do. In this way the client had remained in an idealised state of youthful freedom and irresponsibility. Simultaneously my client was clearly suffering from continually depressive emotionlessness, abandonment, and a lack of drive and was struggling with his professional stagnation. He wanted to continue with his education and reach a new level, for which he, however, did not have the energy. We had worked together then for more than a year, which had proved itself to be relatively challenging, because on the one hand the client was vehemently against considering his cannabis abuse critically, while on the other hand it seemed impossible to influence his recurring depressive conditions. A good therapeutic working relationship, however, had developed between us and the client came gladly to the sessions. He also began increasingly introducing topics which he was currently emotionally concerned with to the psychotherapy (for example, current romantic relationships). With this background, my client then had the following dream, which he, visibly agitated, related in the next therapy session:

I am in an unknown country and am treated very harshly by people, whose nationality I cannot determine. They strip me of my clothes and paint on me with a kind of bright paint, or it could also be clay or mud. Then they hit me and poke me with small sticks, which is very painful. They seize my arms and legs and drag me through the dust until finally we come to a kind of altar. On this altar is a big stone with a round hole in it. My whole body is pushed backwards through this hole by the men, which is also very painful. Afterwards, however, the people are very friendly to me; they dance a joyful dance around me, carry me in their arms, and we go to a kind of feast, in which I am celebrated. Now I feel very accepted and euphoric.

The dream, which for an impartial observer seems initially somewhat unique, had a massive impact on me: I was so affected that I could hardly speak. I was engaged at this time with an inquiry into ethnology and the initiation rituals of different peoples. It suddenly occurred to me that my client's dream described in detail elements of initiation rituals that can be found in different societies, for example in East Africa. If I had not been concerned at this time with the corresponding ethnographical literature, the connection would perhaps not have been so clear to me. What is interesting, is that my client's dream described with mostly accurate details these initiation rituals, although I can with a limited degree of certainty, say that my client did not possess any related knowledge nor had come into contact with any literature on the subject. Moreover, it was extremely interesting that the initiation process in the dream was in principle exactly the kind that my client in his situation at the time needed. Tribal initiation rituals also serve the purpose of allowing adolescents to transition from childhood to adulthood. The partly painful and also frightening procedures which the initiates must undergo, serve the purpose in the eyes of traditional tribes, insofar as ethnology can reconstruct this, of 'killing the child in the person', so as to ease the departure from and the letting go of childish connections, especially to the mother, but also more generally from the original family. Only when the child in the person is put to one side in this way, according to the understanding of ethnology, can the adolescent find the space in himself to get his bearings in the world and to take on both adult values and responsibility in this adult world. Many initiation rituals thus contain the process of a symbolic rebirth or new birth, for example through baptism, through immersion, a submersion in water, in which the old person dies and a re-emergence as a new person, a newborn human, here an adult. In my client's dream this was being pulled through the stone's 'birth canal' on the altar. The altar in the dream thereby signified that a sort of sacred context was being dealt with. It is also typical of initiation rituals that the initiated person is celebrated after they have withstood the difficult procedures of the initiation, proved themselves to be brave, to have endured pain and fear, as well as their inclusion in the adult community, and for whom ordinarily follows a period of instruction of the rules and knowledge of the elders.

This dream of exactly this point of treatment was for me therefore also so intriguing because an initiation was in effect precisely what was needed by my client. Based on his earlier experiences of loss it was not possible for him in a timely manner to disengage from the people attached to his childhood and to dismiss them. He conserved instead the connection to the parents through the life in their 'mausoleum' and continually constructed with his cannabis consumption a sort of trance-like connection to his parents on the other side. The whole thing elevated beyond rationality by the value he placed upon youthful freedom and lack of responsibility. From my position as psychotherapist, what was required here was a bidding fare-well to childhood, which of course would have meant diverging from the usual initiation rituals and the mourning of previous losses, as well as a conscious step into adult responsibility for his life.

When I had become conscious of this connection, I explained to my client at length about initiation rituals and their function in different tribes. Even when this made sense to him, it did not of course effect an immediate profound change in him. For me, however, the dream gave a clear indication of the further development and direction of the therapy, and it was also possible to observe that following the dream it felt easier to address more difficult topics with the client, for example the conservation of mementos of his parents or his excessive cannabis consumption. The therapy continued on for about another two years, in which the client finally managed to get to grips with the loss of his parents, overcome his depressive phases, begin a new apprenticeship, and finally move out of his parents' house and into a more appropriate, smaller apartment. All in all, the result of the therapy was in this way very successful.

The initiation that emerged in my client's dream and which he had to go through, can rightly be identified as an archetype. This example contains the essential elements which constitute the concept of the archetype: it is a universal model that can be found with a similar structure in all time periods and amongst all peoples; it emerges spontaneously from the unconscious, just as here it does in a dream. Ordinarily it can be assumed that the person has no knowledge or experience of the model and it seems to be almost invested in the person. The emergence of the archetype is connected with a psychological energy which causes a transformation – with the initiation it relates to causing the transition from childhood to adulthood. In this way archetypes, especially in transformation processes, like, for example, in psychotherapy, expose themselves as spontaneous expressions of the mind which bring the blocked processes of the mind back into motion and develop a healing effect. Often the emergence makes one awestruck, which Carl Gustav Jung denoted as 'numinosum'. Jung formulated the concept of the archetype for psychology. This conception and its further developments, as well as the areas to which he applied his ideas, are the subjects of this book.

2 The classic definition and theory of Jung's concept of archetypes

The term archetype, in combination with the term 'collective unconscious' and the individuation process, is surely the central concept of Carl Gustav Jung's analytical psychology. The archetypes form the theoretical foundations of Jungian psychology. They distinguish it from other schools of psychotherapy and essentially define the specific approach in psychotherapy with its various methods of dream interpretation, working with images and other symbolic material, active imagination, and so on. The concept of archetypes was – alongside personal conflicts – a main reason for the theoretical differences and the resulting separation of Sigmund Freud and Jung, and marks the beginning of the formation of Jung's own psychological theory (Kirsch 2000).

2.1 Definition

The term archetype is best translated as primordial image (*Urbild*). For Jung, these images belong to the configuration of the human psyche (Jung's own publications on the concept of the archetype can be found in volume 9.1 of the collected works). Archetypes are structural elements of the collective psyche and give psychic energy a defined form, which alone is formless and imperceptible. As contentless shaping factors they form the basis of every experience and perform human experiences, ideas, and actions. Archetypes centre around the fundamental and general experiences of life, such as birth,

DOI: 10.4324/9781003058458-2

marriage, motherhood, death, separation, crises, and so on. They have the following characteristics:

1 According to Jung's understanding, archetypes are inherent patterns of experience and behaviour, which he parallels with the instincts of animals (for further discussion of the innateness of archetypes see Chapter 4.3.1). They are a priori forms of perception and organisation of people's experience of the world, which means they direct and shape the way people encounter their environments. As an example, we could consider the idea that a child is able to see a caregiver as a mother or motherly not only because this person behaves in a certain way, but also because the child possesses a disposition to organise the experience of this person in a certain way, in this case as a mother. Here it is clear that Jung explicitly rejects the notion of behaviourism and learning theory, which at the time was gaining popularity and in the following centuries practically dominated scientific psychology, namely the idea that a child is a 'tabula rasa', or a blank canvas. This implies that at birth a child possesses no specific characteristics or pre-structure, but rather that everything, which later constitutes the psyche, comes through experience and learning. Here Jung was firmly of a different opinion and his psychology denotes almost the antithesis of behaviourism. His concept of archetypes purports that people are already shaped at birth by some profound knowledge, as well as in some ways how they organise psychological experience. This notion of the psyche manifests itself over the course of a lifetime in typical human behaviour, for example, the tendency to commit to a partner monogamously, to formalise this through the ritual of marriage, and to start a family on this basis. This basic configuration of the human psyche leads to human behaviour, development patterns, rituals, symbols, and beliefs that are present in all peoples throughout time.

2 This is synonymous with the fact that archetypes are universal and are, therefore, independent of culture and can be found in the same form in the behaviour as well as

the beliefs and the inner psychological experiences of all people, regardless of location and at all times throughout history.

3　According to Jung, archetypes are strongly affectively charged, which means that when we experience them, they relate to specific and clearly traceable emotions. It could even be said that they structure and channel emotions. When we have archetypal experiences, we experience these frequently as, to use Jung's term, 'numinous'; therefore, they are somehow powerful, sublime, and even frightening. We are in this way overwhelmed by the experience and feel the same sort of reverence as we do when confronted with religious things. The experience appears to be impressive and overpowering, even close to superhuman. A good example of this is the experience of the initiation in my client's dream, described in the introduction, which made a great impression on him as well as myself.

4　Archetypes are unconscious: they come from the unconscious and impact from the unconscious our conscious experience. Jung even assumes that the archetype is never in itself accessible to human consciousness, only its manifestations in the form of pictures, symbols, and so on.

5　Archetypes are autonomous, above all in relation to consciousness. The conscious Ego can neither make nor control them, but rather they spring from the unconscious, out of which they spontaneously emerge, which directs and structures the impact they have on consciousness.

6　Archetypes express themselves frequently in the form of symbols, but also manifest themselves in the form of human actions and behaviours, social phenomena, and other ways. For an extended account of the symbolic terms in analytical psychology, see Dorst (2014).

An example is the symbol of the cross: representations of the cross can be found as early as the Neolithic period and in many cultures across the world and in a variety of epochs it can be found as a religious symbol, for example, with the Teutons in the form of the swastika (a symbol of worshipping the sun), just as in India, of course as the central symbol of the Christian West, and also in cave and rock paintings of the aboriginals in Australia. In the modern age the cross could also, however, capture the attention of the masses and induce veneration outside of religion, in the form of the swastikas of National Socialism. Evidently the cross expresses something very profound and thrilling, which is difficult to fully grasp with words. This is precisely what characterises an archetype.

At this point it must be emphasised that, for Jung's classic definition of the archetype, in his fully differentiated conception, Jung points out that the archetype as such is empty of content and only a general structure is represented, which organises content or information. It could also be called a general attractor. To illustrate this aspect, Jung uses the picture of the structure of a crystal: when a solid body crystallises in a solution, the form or structure of this solid object will be unique and individual, but at the molecular level the crystal lattice is always the same.

> Their form is comparable with the lattice system of crystal, some of which performs in certain ways the structure of the crystal in the mother liquor (the archetype per se), without itself having a material existence. This existence appears first in the manner of the shooting of ions and molecules. The lattice system determines simply the biometric structure, but not the concrete form of the individual crystal [...] and just as the archetype possess [...] a invariable central meaning, which constantly only in principle and not in a concrete form, determines how it appears.
>
> (Jung CW 9/1, p. 95)

2.2 Archetypes in the life of the individual

Archetypical models are waiting to manifest themselves in a Personality. They are capable of taking on an infinite number of variations and are dependent on individuals. They exert a fascination, which is intensified by culturally and traditionally dependent expectations. They are, therefore, bearers of a strong and possibly overwhelming quantity of energy, which, dependent on the developmental stage and level of consciousness – is hard to withstand. Archetypes awaken emotions, make us blind to reality, and take hold of the will. Archetypal living means living without boundaries (Inflation). To declare something archetypal can mean a conscious interaction with a collective and historic image, which gives room for the interplay of elementary polarities: past and present, Personal and collective, typical and unique (contrasts).

(Samuels, Shorter & Plaut 1986, p. 48)

This passage from the *Dictionary of Jungian Psychology* addresses many important aspects of the term archetype. Jung was of the opinion that manifested in archetypes is a transcendental level of meaning for the human existence which wants to be expressed. In this sense, particular archetypes would represent for each person particular issues in their life, which this person must confront at various times and on different levels. Archetypes would be in this sense issues of human existence. Jung tried with this term to find an explanation for why some people must grapple with certain, even distressing, issues. The post-Jungian James Hillman (1983) intensified this later in his *Archetypal Psychology* when he said that life consists of the actualising of the archetypal essence, which is located inside a person. Jung had also taken into account with this term, which is also discernible in the above quotation, that many people are seized in almost excessive ways by an archetype or that they identify with it, what is defined in analytical psychology as 'inflation'. This can, for example, manifest itself in that a person identifies so intensely with the archetype of justice and solidarity with the oppressed, that they rebel against the existing authority and resort to violence and finally perish as a result of this identification. The concept of inflation was an early attempt by Jung to explain individual psychopathology. Jung had already begun his clinical career in psychiatry and had revolutionised psychiatric treatment with the concept that a hidden meaning must lie in the formation of the fantasies

of a psychotic patient, and it is not a case of a fully mean-
ingless production of an organically ill brain. For psychotics,
according to Jung, a massive inflation has taken place, therefore
consciousness can no longer effectively separate itself from the
contents of the unconscious, in particular from the archetypes.
Archetypal content then forces its way into and floods consciousness, in some way completely taking over control of the
personality. In this way psychotic hallucinations can be very
well explained. The question in an analytical psychotherapy
would be then: with which archetype do you profoundly identify with? Which archetype unconsciously defines your life,
without you being distanced from it enough? A psychotherapy
would then revolve around first recognising as an archetype the
motive which is directing the person in order to reflectively distance and disidentify that person from this motive. This would
be a conscious struggle with the archetype playing a role in
the patient's life, and in a successful psychotherapy this aspect
would eventually be integrated as a consciously reflected part of
their own personality, instead of an unconscious driving force.
Jung's opinion on this was frequently laconic: people are not
gods; to identify with them only causes damage. It is illustrated
more fully in Chapter 5.2.1 that it is actually possible to empirically detect the life-defining archetypal models of this kind in
people's biographies.

Finally, another essential aspect of archetypes is addressed
in the above quotation, namely that they are constituted of
opposites. That the psyche is constructed of opposites was one
of Jung's basic assumptions about the human psyche. In his
association studies in the psychiatric clinic at the University of
Zurich, he was able to prove this empirically, in that he identified both the introverted and the extroverted dimensions of
the personality. Jung was convinced that for every characteristic, for every psychic quality, every feature of a personality of
a human being, there was an antithesis and that psychic energy
forms out of the tension between these two poles. The greatest
overall polarity in the psyche should serve well as an example
for this, specifically that between men and women. This energy
manifests itself in the dynamic of love and hate, attraction and

separation, connection and autonomy between the genders. Although it is true that Jung himself did not specifically do it, in principle it is possible to formulate archetypal psychology as a list of central contrasts which constitute the human psyche and by extension human existence. What follows is a list – although by no means an exhaustive one – illustrating such central antithetical pairings in human life:

Antithetical pairings on the bodily level:

- Breathing in–Breathing out
- Waking–Sleeping
- Working–Recovering
- Systole–Diastole

Antithetical pairings on the psychic and relationship level:

- Closeness–Distance
- Devotion–Distancing
- Dependence–Independence
- Weakness–Strength
- Submission–Dominance (power)
- Superiority–Inferiority (self-worth)
- Community–Self-will
- Introversion–Extroversion
- Transition–Consistency
- Irrational–Rational
- Feeling–Reason
- Letting go–Control
- Acceptance–Confrontation
- Cooperation–Competition
- Coalescence–Separation

In mythology and religious stories, we find these archetypal antithetical pairings personified in the shape of gods and mythical creatures or heroes. In analytical psychology, therefore, there is also an intense preoccupation with mythology, comparative religious studies, ethnology, and comparative cultural studies because through psychological analysis of such mythical figures, insights into basic qualities, even archetypal characteristics, of the human psyche can be gained. An example: among the figures of the gods, who in the imagination of the ancient Greeks inhabited Mount Olympus, is the goddess of love, Aphrodite, officially married to Hephaestus, the god of blacksmithing and of craftsmanship. She actually has, however, a secret relationship with the god of war, Mars. In a famous myth, Hephaestus manages to catch both of them in the act of love in a metal net and brings them before the gods, so that they can laugh at them with the famous Olympic laughter. The psychologically interesting substance of this myth is, however, that there is a secret connection or attraction between love and aggression. It could be interpreted that it does a romantic relationship good to contain a certain amount of aggression, whether this is a good demarcation from each other, or perhaps also in a certain measure of conflict, which is consciously dealt with. The Jungian Peter Schellenbaum (1994) has explained this further.

Jung also developed a method in order to identify or at least to narrow down the psychological content of archetypes. This method is defined as 'amplification'. In this method all cultural parallels for a certain archetypal motive or symbol are gathered, so use of the archetype in different cultures, in mythology, in religious beliefs, and so on, in order to define the field of meaning of the archetypal symbol. In the practice of Jungian psychology, defined lexica of symbols will as a rule be used, which does not allocate a clear meaning to a symbol, but instead gives an overview of the usage of a symbol in different cultures, religions, traditions, and so on. Fairy tales and myths are also used in this way (see Chapter 5.1). The amplification of an archetypal symbol does not revolve around determining a wholly specific meaning for a symbol, but rather around bringing meanings into fluctuation by exposing the field of meaning in the person, who is engaged with the archetype.

> The basic principles, the archetypes, of the unconscious are, because of their evocativeness, indescribable, despite being recognisable. The intellectual judgement always seeks, naturally, to assess their uniqueness and thus get

past the essence, because above all the only thing about their nature which can be assessed, is their ambiguity, their almost immeasurable wealth of meaning, which each clear formulation makes impossible.

(Jung CW 9/1, p. 80)

2.3 Manifestations of archetypes

Archetypes can manifest themselves on many different levels and in different forms:

1 Primitive Perception Mode: It was already mentioned above that all newborn humans come into the world with an expectation: the experience of a motherly figure or to be mothered. This manifests itself concretely in the infant's search for the mother's breast immediately after birth. Newborns must, therefore, not learn this activity but rather come with this already preformed expectation. This would be an example for a clear, biologically rooted, primitive mode of how the human essence organises the experience of the world. Research has confirmed that all human infants build an attachment to at least one adult caregiver and that the model of connection formed through this is universal (Stevens 1983, 2003). In much the same way, the early ability of recognising faces, the special attention newborns give to human stimuli, for example, the human voice amongst others (see Knox 2003), can be similarly categorised.

2 Images and Shapes: The cross was mentioned above as an example of an abstract form with archetypal character. Another symbol frequently used by Jung as an abstract model is the so-called mandala, a term which originates from Tibetan Buddhism. There, as part of many kinds of ceremonies an abstract image, whose basic form is usually round or square and is inverted on various axes, is drawn out of coloured sand on the floor. Tibetan Buddhists understand a mandala to represent the strange order of things, and it frequently serves as an object for meditation as something

to achieve inner centring and order. The same idea can be found on the other side of the world, specifically with the Navaho Indian tribe in the southwestern USA. There, in ritual ceremonies to heal illnesses or mental disturbances, shamans carry out the drawing of an image out of multi-coloured sand on the floor, frequently accompanied by ceremonial singing. There are various basic patterns of these sand drawings which are intended for various purposes, for example, as healing ceremonies for different problems and disturbances, and which must be learned by the shaman of this tribe during his training, just as with the accompanying chants. Here too, the sand drawing, which is also normally circular, serves the purpose of being an experience of the strange order of things and the affected ill people should, through their participation in the ceremony and observation of the image in the sand, find a renewed centre and inner order. Finally, a similar idea can be found in Western Christian society, namely in the artistic, colourful, and circular rose windows in Gothic cathedrals. Here too, the idea was that the window, through its shape and form, conveyed an expression of God's heaven, along also with the strange order, and made it visible to believers. And yet, it can be assumed that these cultures surely had hardly any exchange over these kind of concepts.

3 Living Entities and Objects: In many cultures, certain animals, plants, and inanimate objects have coinciding symbolic meanings. Birds, for example, are regarded in many cultures as manifestations of the spirit, and therefore shamans and healers in various cultures traditionally adorn themselves with bird feathers because this expresses their connection to the spirit world. In the same way, the tree coincides in many cultures as a symbol of the evolution of man, as well as of the connection between the earth and the sky. As an example of an animal with an archetypal meaning, the snake should here be mentioned. In ancient Greece, the snake entwined around a rod was the symbol of the god Asclepius, who was worshipped as the god of medicine. The symbol of the snake wound around a staff

still adorns pharmacies today. This symbol is also found in the Old Testament with the same meaning, namely in the shape of the bronze snake in the second book of Moses. At God's command, Moses erected a bronze snake which the Israelites should look up to in order to be cured of an unknown illness that had afflicted them in the desert. In many other cultures the snake is seen as a symbol of healing processes, or indeed more generally for transformation, perhaps because the snake regularly sheds its skin and emerges each time anew.

4   Social patterns, rules, and rituals: The initiation ritual was mentioned above as an example of a ritual with archetypal characteristics. Now a further pattern, or more particularly ritual, as an example for an archetype will be explained, specifically marriage. We find in all peoples on the planet and in every different epoch, from primitive conditions of living traditional tribes to the highly differentiated late-modern societies, coinciding examples of the model of social behaviour in which a man and a woman join together as a pair in a way which is ritualised and regulated by the human collective. Ethnologists have moreover established that there are astonishing similarities in the rules and ritual proceedings of marriages in many cultures. The French ethnographer Claude Lévi-Strauss (1976) discovered such a similarity in the rule present in many traditional tribes in completely different parts of the earth, which can be denoted as the 'Uncle Rule'. Before the actual ritual of the marriage, the brother of the mother of the bride (the uncle) leads the bride out of her parents' house and brings her to her groom. It can also be assumed here, that these different cultures surely had hardly any cultural exchange about the specific rules and rituals of this kind.

5   Narrative Models: Stories in the form of fairy tales, myths, and legends can also have archetypal character – 'Gods are metaphors for archetypal behaviour, myths are archetypal scenes' (Samuels et al. 1986, p. 48). Jung himself had already previously hinted that fairy tales represent an embodiment of archetypes in narrative form. Most prominently his

pupil Marie-Louise von Franz (1986) has been intensively concerned with the examination of the archetypal content of fairy tales and has described their use in psychotherapy. In his book *Transformations and Symbols of the Libido* from 1912 (Jung CW 5), which was the trigger for his break with Freud, Jung had concerned himself extensively with the psychotic fantasies of a young woman, which he came upon in her diary entries. At the heart of the book is the argument that these fantasies run parallel to mythological motifs. Jung could especially identify the myth of the hero in these various fantasy images. The motif of the hero, who bravely sets out on a great journey in order to free his people or even the whole world from a threat, for example, a dragon, pervades the fairy tales and myths of all peoples. In this way, the myth of the hero can be defined as an archetypal narrative.

6   Religious and philosophical ideas, world views, political ideologies: Archetypal structures can also be found on the level of abstract ideas, world views, and convictions. Here the motif of death and resurrection shall be used as an example. The earliest form of this religious idea taken down in writing can be found as early as ancient Egypt in the myth of the death and the dismemberment of the god Osiris by his adversary Seth. The sister of Osiris, Isis, collects the dismembered limbs and puts them together and she buries the dead brother, who then comes back to life and sires with her the son Horus. The same motif of death and resurrection can moreover be found in the old Persian religion of Zarathustra in the myth of the Phoenix, which rises from the ashes, and of course in the Christian belief in the death and resurrection of Christ. In ancient Greece, the most meaningful religious event was the Eleusinian Mysteries, which were repeated every year. It is not known in detail how these events proceeded because the participants of the mysteries were strictly sworn to silence. Today, however, it is assumed that at the centre of the mysteries a grain kernel was buried, out of which a sprout emerged, and this was taken as a promise of a life after death for the adept.

At the high point of the mystery the following words were apparently said by the leading priest: 'Whoever dies before he dies, does not die when he dies'.

7   Mental Processes: Finally, developments in the human psyche, particularly transformation processes, can also have an archetypal nature. The central example for this is the individuation process, which is archetypally invested in every person and inclines towards bringing about, over the course of the person's life, the expression of the person's individuality and moving the personality in the direction of its totality (see in greater detail Chapter 2.5).

The above description of ways in which archetypes can manifest is an attempt to systematise and conceptualise the different descriptions of and discourses about archetypes in the literature of analytical psychology. Simultaneously though, a problem, which will be more fully engaged with later, becomes clear, namely that the use of the term archetype in analytical psychology can itself be described as inflationary, as will be clear in, for example, the following statement from the *Dictionary of Jungian Psychology* (Samuels et al. 1986, p. 48): 'The number of archetypes is theoretically unlimited'. To some extent, the levels explained above drastically differentiate themselves from each other, and it remains unclear what indeed constitutes the core of an archetype and how it will be conveyed. From my point of view, this problem in analytical psychology remains to be solved. Jung himself has indeed contributed to this problem through his use of the term.

2.4 The collective unconscious

The concept of the collective unconscious absolutely belongs to the term archetype. Jung assumes that in addition to the personal unconscious, as it is described by Freud, the collective unconscious also exists, a mental inheritance for humanity of which all people have a part. This collective unconscious contains the archetypes and is precisely in this way collective, because the archetypes are universal and consequently shared by all people. The collective unconscious is structured through the totality of the existing archetypes and possess in this way an inner order. In Jung's psychology a positive role in human development is attributed to the unconscious in general and particularly the collective unconscious. Especially during crises and mental disturbances, according to Jung, the unconscious makes archetypal images and structures available for consciousness in order to give indications for a new alignment or centring. In this sense, archetypes contain the fundamental patterns for the personality's healing process, which become effective in crises, troubles, and situations in which the psyche has slid out of balance. These archetypes become made available in different ways: on the one hand, in dreams, daydreams and visions, or spontaneous fantasies; on the other hand, the process of activating archetypes can actively be initiated, for example, in the context of therapy, by stimulating the client to create pictures or other images in which unconscious content comes to be expressed. Finally, the symptoms of mental crises or disturbances also contain indications of the underlying archetype. In this way the archetype can heal effectively through an embodiment of the entirety of the antithetical pair. Has the personality or the conscious Ego become one-sided, for example, extensively rational, it would then be expected that the unconscious activates the antithesis of the corresponding archetype and this could then manifest itself so that the affected person developed symptoms of pronounced irrationality. This would contain within itself at the same time the expression of the imbalance of the conscious personality, as well as also the solution, that which was missing or underdeveloped.

In later years, and in particular in his discourse with the quantum physicist Wolfgang Pauli on the so-called Unus Mundus, Jung further developed this concept of the collective unconscious, the contents of which are archetypes as contrasting pairs or polarities. By this, Jung means the hypothesis of a unified reality, which lies behind or underlies experienced reality, that contains in it all entities in their entirety, thus encompassing all oppositions, albeit only potentially. In principle this hypothesis of a unified reality is a transcendental conception; therefore, Jung defines it also as a 'Psychoid', or only 'psyche-like'. This unified reality manifests itself then in the experienced reality, although here only one polarity of the opposition can be realised. A relationship of tension emerges in opposition to that not yet realised, only potentially present antithesis, which in principle is the development of the psyche that drives forward the whole of life. Jung closely based this concept on the formation of theories in quantum physics, as they were known at the time. In recent times these conceptions have been further developed in the form of generalised quantum theories (for more extensive coverage of this topic, see Roesler 2013, 2015).

2.5 The individuation process

The concept of the individuation process likewise belongs to the notion of archetype. This process can also be viewed as archetypal. Jung makes the assumption that there is a tendency invested in the human psyche to move, throughout the course of life, towards the potential wholeness of the personality and simultaneously bring into being the individuality of the personal character. 'I use the expression Individuation in the sense of that process which generates a psychological individual, which means a separate, indivisible, and whole individual' (Jung CW 9/1, p. 490). In the centre of the psyche an archetypal structure, which Jung describes as the Self, can be assumed. This Self would be a kind of structure which expresses wholeness as well as individual uniqueness. Insofar as the Self is at the same time the centre of the person as well as its totality, it is a paradoxical description which Jung, however, consciously makes. The concept of the Self here would also be a very clear example that Jung conceptualised archetypes as transcendent.

Over the course of a person's life, a movement comes out from the Self, which confronts the person with a number of archetypal stations with both life issues and conflicts. In the process of these conflicts, an ever greater sense of individuality forms and the personality succeeds increasingly in integrating the as yet unrealised parts or potentials of the person. In the second half of his life, Jung principally focused his attention on this individuation process, its progression, and its typical stages, and he dedicated the largest portion of his time to research into this process. His preoccupation with alchemy, its ideas, images, and concepts, delivered for him indications into the archetypal structure of this process.

2.5.1 *The two halves of life and the midlife crisis*

This process is initially divided into two halves: the first half of a person's life is about adjusting the personality to fit with the outside demands and the social reality, therefore to develop a stable identity or a clear orientation in life (e.g., a choice of career, training, and the expansion of professional skills and competencies), to learn social rules and also behavioural roles, to become capable of relationships, and potentially to start a family. Altogether it is possible to say that in this first half of the processes an adjustment to the social community and the demands of the outside reality should take place. Nevertheless, an inevitable imbalance develops during this first half of the process. On the one hand, practically everyone brings with them talents or abilities in certain areas as well as specific biases to certain activities or occupations, which will as a rule be particularly strongly trained because of the need to align with a demand for achievement in the first half of life. On the other hand, this process will also be supported by social authorities, for example, parents, and moreover educators and other guiding figures can, based on their own personal preferences or evaluations, emphasise certain qualities in the growing personality. All this eventually leads to other qualities, characteristics, and potentials of the personality, which are not supported in this way but that are at least potentially inherent in the person, remaining unconscious or unrecognised or even being repressed. This is in Jung's opinion initially a totally natural process, which can, however, if the imbalances are particularly intense or the tension between the lived and unlived is particularly big, take on the intensity of a neurosis. Jung comments in relation to this that the neurotic person is a person split in two.

Jung's discovery was now that in the clients who came to him for treatment, he regularly noticed a crisis in the middle of their lives, in which the person's path of development and also the orientation and values that they had appropriated were fundamentally called into question. In extreme cases, the affected patients will call the meaning of their lives into question. This phenomena, referred to by Jung as the midlife crisis, has by now become so well known that the term, above all in English, has passed over into general conversational usage. This crisis for Jung is, however, no accident or disturbance, but rather an essential part of the individuation process as described here. In the middle of life, when the alignment to the outside demands and realities should have been achieved and the person has established both their role models and themselves in their social contexts, a retrograde process sets in, and in the psyche the question emerges of to what extent the external alignments and achievements are really essential for the person and what they will outlast. Jung gets to the heart of the tendency in his formulation: 'Am I related to eternity?'

As has been previously stated, Jung was above all interested in this second half of the individuation process for the greatest part of his work, and had also tried to describe the contents and patterns of the process in a generally applicable form through his work with psychotherapy patients as well as through comparative cultural research.

In what follows, the archetypal stages of the individuation process in their typical sequence will be described (a summary can be found in Jung (1928/1989) 'The Relationship between the Ego and the Unconscious', CW 7).

2.5.2 The Persona

In the first half of the individuation process described above and its emphasis on the alignment with social and external requirements, a part of the personality develops which Jung describes as the Persona (from the Latin *Personare* – to sound through). The Persona serves as something like a mask for the personality, in the sense that role models and established and partly schematic patterns of behaviour are vital for the personality to function in professional or social contexts. It is critical to emphasise that Jung does not describe such a behavioural role using a mask as something to be condemned or disturbed, but rather he views it as virtually essential. Nevertheless, the Persona will encounter problems when it is overemphasised in the personality, and as a result an overwhelming alignment to the outside has taken place and the Ego has lost the connection to the deepest levels of the personality, to its own essence. This was, at least in Jung's time, a frequent reason why patients sought him out in order to have psychotherapy. An overemphasis of the Persona and a loss of the relationship to one's own interior will be frequently experienced by those affected as, according to Jung, a loss of meaning, and it can be detected in a variety of symptoms, for example, depression, or can also lead to unconscious actions in the sense of an attempt to break away from one's restrictive role, for example, in the form of erotic affairs which bring about the stated crisis. In this sense the emergence of the midlife crisis is a necessary and ultimately also meaningful condition because at this point the person can no longer evade their own self-realisation and the engagement with their own interior and own essence.

2.5.3 The shadow

At this point in the crisis, if the person consciously engages with the conflict, for example, as part of psychotherapy, the conflict with the so-called 'shadow' emerges as the next stage of the individuation process. Jung defined the shadow as all the elements of a personality which have been so far evaluated as worthless, damaging, or distressing by consciousness and have been repressed or even separated as a result. Shadow encompasses all those things which belong to us and which we as personal characteristics or features experience, but which we are ashamed of or consciously reject (e.g., greed, aggression, avarice). Jung defined the shadow simply as that which a person 'does not desire to be' (Jung CW 16, p. 470). The formation of the shadow is of course strongly influenced through the process of socialisation.

Ordinarily a person learns through their upbringing or more generally through the overall alignment with social norms and values in the process of the first half of the individuation process, which qualities and characteristics are desired and accepted and which are not. In this way the traces of one's upbringing, the strictness, rejection, criticism which have been experienced in the childhood or youth from the carer or educator and have been internalised, can be found in the shadow. With the concept of the shadow, Jung always honourably underscored Freud's contribution to the investigation of the personal unconscious, and in principle Jung's shadow can be equated with Freud's repressed. Jung clearly emphasises more than Freud, however, that in the shadow there is also always an unlived value, a potential. In the course of the individuation process, the conflict with the shadow is about recognising the value of things previously repressed and in this process to transform their own measurements of value, to develop things previously rejected, and to integrate them into the personality.

The shadow as an archetype forms an archetypal contrasting pair with the Persona as its antithesis. The Persona and the shadow are interrelated in the sense that all that which the Persona has rejected and faded out falls into the possession of the shadow and does not disappear, but rather contains its own dynamic. Afterwards, the shadow parts of the personality press to be allowed to coexist (Kast 1999). As has been mentioned above, this dynamic becomes relevant particularly in the midlife crisis and at the beginning of the individuation process in the second half of life. The problem of the shadow can be overcome, as long as it is unconscious, with the mechanism of projection; hence, the characteristics rejected by the person will be ascribed to others and then judged or even persecuted. This is probably one of the most well-established mechanisms of how humans regulate their own identity and their own self-worth amongst others. Shadow projections can also be experienced collectively and have extremely destructive consequences, a prominent example of which is European anti-Semitism, which peaked in the extermination of millions of Jewish people during the period of National Socialism. Fundamentally, all xenophobia, and indeed more broadly the idea of a scapegoat, can coherently be explained with the problem of the shadow and its projection.

With severely unconscious shadow parts, there is the additional danger that through a loss of conscious control they suddenly break into conscious behaviour and here they will ordinarily have a destructive impact. Sudden aggressive outbreaks from people who otherwise are very well adjusted and controlled are a typical example of this. It is known that those people who commit mass shootings, killing both other people and often themselves in an outburst of violence, were frequently very unremarkable and well-adjusted people. Such a phenomenon can be explained with Jung's concept of the shadow. For the treatment of one's own shadow, Jung gave the quite serious advice: every day a bad deed. This serves as a reminder that one should continually be aware of one's shadow and ultimately to make an effort to give it a place in one's own life.

> Everybody is pursued by a shadow and the less this is embodied in the conscious life of the individual, the blacker it is and tighter it clings to us. When we are conscious of an inferiority, there is always the chance to correct it. If it is also constantly in contact with other interests, it is constantly subject to change. But when it is isolated and pushed out of consciousness, it will never be corrected. Out of this, then, comes the danger that in an instant of unawareness the repressed will suddenly break out. In every case it forms an unconscious obstacle that causes the best-intentioned efforts to failure.
>
> (Jung CW 11, p. 131)

Alongside this personal shadow, analytical psychology identifies moreover an archetypal shadow. Here, Jung is referring to a general tendency towards evil and destruction present in everybody. This archetypal or collective shadow, the general evil, forms another archetypal contrasting pair with good. With this concept Jung attempted to indicate that we as people at all times and in all cultures must face evil and that a fully good being as such does not exist. This necessary duality in every image of God is the central theme of Jung's book *Answer to Job* (Jung CW 11), in which he grapples with the suppression of evil in the Christian conception of God. In cultural and religious stories, this general evil is frequently expressed as the devil or Satan, or it appears in the representation of witches, demons, evil spirits, and so on. The characterisation of it as an archetype is in this way justified, as there is practically no religion or religious system which does not contain a concept of absolute evil.

2.5.4 The image of the soul: Anima and Animus

The next archetypal stage on the way to individuation represents the encounter with the so-called soul image. Jung postulates that present in every person's inner soul is a counterpart of the opposite gender which, seen psychologically, has the task of conferring between consciousness and unconscious. For a man, therefore, this soul image has a feminine character and is described as an Anima. For a woman, it takes on a male character and is described as Animus. In principle, just the claim that every human carries with them a part of their inner psyche that is of the opposite gender is one of Jung's epochal contributions to psychology and this, like so many, has descended over time into general knowledge. Anima and Animus each represent archetypes, which means they also each carry in themselves a polarity between positive and negative. Jung postulates that the Anima expressed for a man his emotionality, or more specifically his mindset towards his own emotional life, while the Animus for a woman represents the mental principle or her general mindset and accessibility to mental qualities and substance. This is of course, seen from today's perspective, an extremely problematic statement because it would imply that feelings are not suited to men but are instead something foreign, while for women the same is implied about intellect. Jung's concept of Anima and Animus has been strongly criticised as analytical psychology has developed further and a new conception of this soul image has formed in the course of the debate, which will be presented more extensively in Chapter 2.5.5. At this point it should be noted that Jung's description of these archetypes took the empirical values and cultural norms of his own time as if they were absolute and, it must be clearly stated, he did not really reflect on this. At the same time, it is still the case that encountering this inner image of the opposite gender in the soul and then, above all, developing an attitude in which the image of the soul is taken seriously and a continuous personal relationship is built up with it, represents the decisive stage in the individuation process. If the inner opposite-gender part of the soul, and all that belongs to it, achieves consciousness, it will act as a gateway to the deepest levels of the unconscious.

The Anima for men ordinarily shows itself initially in dreams, as an unknown but fascinating female figure, for example. She has a strong influence on the emotional mood of the man and can in her negative form lead to severe unhappiness, taking the form of a bad mood, emotional instability, or even complete depression. In her positive form, however, she can stimulate, inspire, and produce creative energy. Archetypal images for the Anima in her negative aspect would be witches or destructive temptresses (as clearly shown in the film *The Blue Angel*; a new cinematic depiction of this theme would be *Femme Fatale*). In her positive aspect she would be the lover, muse, and spiritual guide (the most famous example in cultural history is perhaps the figure of Beatrice in Dante's *Divine Comedy*). If the man is successful in building a positive relationship with the Anima and it is integrated as far as possible, this allows him to access his own feelings, his feminine side, his ability to have a relationship, his creative potential, and moreover the centre of his person, the possible Self. Jung describes four different stages in the development of the Anima's image. In the first stage the image is one of a fully biological, earthly femininity, manifested as the original mother or Eve. The Anima in the second stage appears as above all sexually and erotically attractive. Eros is emphasised in the third stage as the image takes on the form of Maria. Finally, in the fourth stage, the image takes on the female form of wisdom, Sophia.

The Animus for a woman also initially shows itself as a fascinating male figure, who is above all attractive on an intellectual level and seems to be influential. Moreover, it is postulated in analytical psychology that the Animus has the tendency to appear in multiple numbers. In its negative form the Animus creates for the woman irrational opinions and beliefs which are then almost violently represented. In its positive aspect it opens the path for the woman to the intellectual world and to her intellectual potential. Archetypal images of the negative aspect of the Animus are mythical figures like killers of women, for example, Bluebeard in fairy tales, and for the positive aspect, heroic figures like the noble knight Lancelot or intellectual and religious leaders like Mahatma Gandhi. Just as Jung had himself differentiated the development of the Anima image into four different stages, his wife, Emma Jung (1967), also undertook the same for the development of the Animus. She also differentiated four aspects or stages. In the first stage, the Animus embodied power, for example, in the figure of the outdoorsman or adventurer. In the second stage, the Animus appears as action, for example, as an energetic hero, sportsman, and so on. In the third stage, it manifests itself as the art of speaking, for example, as a talented speaker, actor, or poet. Finally, in the fourth stage it appears as an intellect, for example, in the form of a guru.

Just as with the shadow, these archetypal images in one's soul often initially appear projected onto other people. This projection of the Anima or Animus generally appears as something equivalent to an intense love and fascination with a person of another gender. In this way the psychology of Anima and Animus are excellently suited to the description of the dynamic in a pair relationship (a very good and comprehensive representation of this classical outlook on Anima/Animus projection can be found in Sanford (1991)). Moreover, Jung emphasises that one's inner soul image is also strongly shaped through the experiences with parents of the opposite gender. The main function of the soul image is, however, in its function as a mediator between the Ego and the inner world, so that the person can be conveyed between the Ego and the outside world.

A large part of Jung's work is intensely concerned with the figure of the Anima and Animus, and the same is true of his immediate students, such as Marie-Louise von Franz, James

Hillman, and others. A central element of this is the meaning of the conflict with the soul image as part of the individuation process. While the conflict with the shadow and attempts to integrate it into consciousness can potentially last an entire lifetime, it is ultimately, however, an easily understandable step in the individuation process. For Jung, and in analytical psychology more broadly, the conflict with and integration of the soul image, on the other hand, is much more demanding and persists for a huge portion of one's life (accordingly Jung characterised the integration of the shadow as a 'Companion piece' and the integration of the Anima/Animus in contrast as a 'Master piece').

2.5.5 Digression: criticism of the Anima–Animus concept and contemporary conceptions

As has been previously mentioned, Jung's conception of the Anima and Animus has been, in part, heavily criticised and controversially discussed in the world of analytical psychology and beyond. Jung's descriptions, which are repeatedly both contradictory and confusing throughout the whole of his work, leave him open to a lot of criticism. In his conception of the soul image as an archetype, the masculine and feminine qualities that he refers to are those of his cultural and time period. He was accused of having served the interests of, in the worst case, sexist and chauvinistic value judgements. From today's standpoint, it is almost unthinkable to suggest that for a woman the intellect is not initially directly accessible or intrinsic and that the same cannot be said about a man and his relationship to his feelings. Various authors in analytical psychology have, therefore, taken the view that Anima and Animus can be regarded as archetypal structures which are present in both genders in the same form and can therefore logically develop in both genders (Hillmann 1981a, Hillman 1981b, Heisig 1996, Kast 1984. For my point of view, this concept would also allow Anima and Animus to respectively be classified as feminine and masculine or, more precisely, to be comprehended as specific mental qualities which are not absolutely connected to men or women. The suggestion has also already been made within analytical psychology to describe these principles with alchemical terms, specifically as Sol and Luna (Schwartz-Salant 1998). This would help solve the confusion between the description of the mental qualities and of real men and women. Annette and Lutz Müller have moreover made an additional suggestion for clarity in their dictionary of Jung's psychology:

> a tentative compromise between the two positions could be to differentiate between a feminine and masculine principle on one side and the Anima/Animus aspect on the other side. If this were the case, femininity as well as masculinity would be found in principle in both genders and in different variations and manifestations for each individual and the terms Anima/Animus remain reserved for each gender specific variant of the principles. The Anima describes, then, the specific entity of all conscious and unconscious feminine aspects in Men and the Animus the specific entity of all conscious and unconscious masculine aspects in women. In this definition, the shared as well as different aspects between men and women could be comprehended.
>
> (Müller & Müller 2003)

A very extensive discussion of this topic can be found in Samuels (1986).

2.5.6 The old sage and the great mother (the mana personalities)

After the conflict with the archetype of the soul image, next the archetypal figures of old sage and the great mother emerge, those figures which are located directly in the environment of the Self, thus the centre of the psyche. The old sage is characterised in the classical Jungian definition as the personification of the intellect, as boundless knowledge and understanding, as wisdom and awareness of the nature of being. The archetype of the great mother, however, is characterised by Jung and his immediate followers as the objective truth of nature or as the archetype of the material principle. Both archetypes are described by Jung as mana personalities, by which the 'extraordinary impactful' is meant. The conflict with these figures, in which in the classical Jungian definition the man must grapple with the old sage, and the woman with the great mother, has an impact in principle on the decided steps towards self-realisation, the conscious realisation of one's own individuality. As part of this, a true detachment from the real parental figures and a realisation respectively of the masculine and feminine identity should occur. The figure of the old sage appears in mythology as well as in personal experience, frequently in the figure of sorcerers, prophets, magicians, or leaders from the underworld. An excellent example from cultural history is the blind seer Teiresias, who leads the hero Odysseus into the underworld as well as indicates for him the way back home (symbolic seen as a return to the Self). The great mother, however, appears as a goddess of fertility, a nymph, priestess, or simply as the embodiment of maternalism, in her spirit form as the Mother Church or Sofia, Mother of Wisdom. The university would be signified as alma mater. The Jung scholar Erich Neumann has conducted a comprehensive cultural historical investigation of the manifestations of the archetype of the great mother (Neumann 1974) and the different forms in which this archetype appears, which can be found in orthodox Christianity, from the primitive beginnings as an animal mistress to the appearance of Sophia as the deepest female knowledge.

Both archetypes contain within them in turn the opposition of the positive and negative poles. The old sage can, therefore, appear in its negative form as an evil sorcerer and magician, or a sinister master of the underworld who holds the psyche under his spell. The great mother appears in her negative aspect as a mother who captures and devours her children, who does not permit her offspring any independence from her. This manifests for example, in the Indian goddess Kali or in the devouring mythological monsters Scylla and Charybdis. Jung had his own personal experience of these archetypal figures. In his struggle with his unconscious, the figure of Philemon appeared to him in his dreams and visions as an old, bearded, wise man and led him through and explained to him his own inner world. An analogue for this can be found in Dante's *Divine Comedy* in the figure of Virgil. Frequently, people project these figures onto real people whom they then honour as intellectual leaders, gurus, or religious teachers. It is also clear here, what tremendous power and influence these figures even in their projection can have over the personality. In extreme form, large numbers of people can be corrupted. This can be clearly seen with fundamentalist terrorism, in which young people under the instruction of a self-proclaimed intellectual leader like, for example, Osama bin Laden (who interestingly was precisely the visual manifestation of the old sage), are ready to even sacrifice their lives. In favourable cases people can achieve self-knowledge and deep religious experience through the projection of these figures onto a supportive teacher or intellectual leader.

Finally, it must also be noted that both of these archetypes are shaped very strongly, particularly in childhood, by the experience of a real mother and father. These are, above all in early childhood, made into god-like figures, who can have an almost unlimited influence on the formation of the child's psyche. Even more important is then, in the course of the individuation process, the detachment of this projection of the mana personalities from the concrete parental figures and their integration into one's own psyche. Otherwise, self-confirmed independence is hardly possible, even as an adult.

We also find the same problem here that we have already seen with the soul image archetypes and their connection with the masculine and feminine genders respectively in the way that Jung posits them. If, as the Jungian scholar Jolande Jacobi has put it, 'the man is matter turned to intellect, the woman is intellect-infused matter, the man's essence is determined by intellect, the woman's by matter' (Jacobi 1986 p. 126), this is from today's perspective highly problematic. These statement repeats what has already been said in relation to Anima and Animus, namely that intellect is allegedly foreign to the essence of the woman. This is why modern Jungians have argued that the archetype of the great mother also includes a principle of wisdom, but under the banner of femininity (Riedel 1989).

She still knows about the archetypal laws of life and is sometimes herself a figure of mother nature. Behind her a godly knowledge still shimmers. The old sage can appear in a variety of shapes, for example as toads, as wise snakes [...] In her darkest form she is contaminated and appears in the form of a witch. Based on her knowledge, however, she can also continually keep her distance from the dark aspects and can therefore come into contact with the heroes and safeguard them against the dark intentions of their opponents. It is proven at the end of each fairy tale: without meeting with these wise, old women the heroes and heroines would not have reached the level of development which they now have [...] She gives no concrete advice on what must be done, but rather brings the heroine – sometimes also a male hero – into their own path of experience. She does not interfere, rather she must be searched for and found. In much the same way as an old wise man, this female sage appears as someone to guide the soul, as a doctor, therapist, as teacher, mistress, priestess, and as a grandmother. The mental aspect of this quality appears as feminine knowledge: knowing about the right herb, the right time, and understanding those things which need to be done [...] What especially distinguishes the old female sage, in contrast to the old wise man, is her especially feminine knowledge about Eros and relationships, which she conveys to the heroine of the fairy story.

(Riedel in Müller & Müller, p. 231)

2.5.7 *The Self*

The last stage of the individuation process is the archetype of the Self, the endpoint of which also simultaneously signals the completion of a self-realisation process, that which is defined as the centre of the psyche and at the same time its totality. 'The Self is not only the centre, but also the whole that encompasses consciousness and unconscious. It is the centre of the mental totality, just as the I is the centre of consciousness' (Jung CW 12, p. 59). This is a paradoxical definition, which Jung has consciously made in order to indicate the numinous and transcendental character of this archetype.

> [The Self] is at once external and inside, totally ourselves and also unrecognisable to us, a virtual middle point of mysterious constitution [...] The beginnings of our whole spiritual life seem to spring inextricably from this point. Our highest and ultimate goals seem to come out of it. It is a paradox that is nevertheless inevitable if we want to label something that is beyond the possibility of our understanding.
>
> (Jung CW 7, p. 260)

In this sense the Self is at once the core of the individuality, the whole uniqueness of the person, and at the same time collective and transcendental, the entirety of the personality, essentially its wholeness, and the realisation of being human as such. In a certain sense the Self is the basis of all archetypes; it is the root archetype, out of which emerge the others as part of the individuation process. The fact that every person carries this archetype in themselves can help us understand the general human desire for religion or religious knowledge and the search for God. One can imagine the Self in this sense as the centre of the psyche where consciousness and the unconscious form a connection and the opposition between the two is balanced. The conflict with the Self mainly conveys the solution to the problem of the opposites, or the connection and balancing out of the opposites, of subjectivity and objectivity, the demands of the outer and inner realities, the transcendental and the concrete, the archetypal and the personal. In this way the Self can be understood as an archetypal image of someone's full potential and the unity of the personality as a whole. Jung's pupil Erich Neumann later developed this theory of the Self to the so-called Ego-Self-Axis. He theorises that in the individuation process, the Ego is connected with the Self in a productive way as the centre of the personality. The Ego then, as the centre of consciousness, always draws from the Self as the centre of the overall psyche and is oriented and renewed from this. This is synonymous with the realisation of one's own individuality, which then shows itself in the Ego.

The term 'the Self', as used by Jung, is intricately connected with the image of god. The Self was frequently denoted by Jung as 'god within us' or 'our part of God'. In the established religions, the symbol of the Self is always synonymous with the image of god. In his work *Aion* (CW 9/2), Jung was intensively concerned with the figure of Christ as a symbol for the Self ('the son of humanity') in Christianity. In this sense it could be possible to equate the experience of meeting or realising the archetype of the Self in religious terms with the concept of enlightenment or a vision of god. Because the Self represents a middle point or the centre of the psyche, the symbol of the Self is also denoted by the corresponding middle point or central representation. The most well-known symbol for the Self, which has been investigated comprehensively by Jung himself, is the aforementioned mandala.

> They are all concerned emphatically with a middle and are located in a circle or a polygon (usually a square) through which the 'totality' is typified. Many of them have flowers, cross, or wheel shapes with clear propensity for multiples of four.
>
> (Jacobi 1965, p. 136)

Symbols or representations which contain the four elements can likewise be described as typical symbols of the Self: the four wind directions of the compass, the four seasons, the four evangelists who surround the figure of Christ, and so on. Typical symbolic representations for the Self are moreover the rose of the Rosicrucian Order, the heavenly city with the quadratic floor plan as a representation of the middle point of paradise (e.g., the heavenly Jerusalem), and so on. In alchemy the central symbol for the Self is the so-called Philosopher's Stone, which allows the 'squaring of the circle' (which is completely mathematically impossible), and by which the unification of opposites is meant. Analogues can also be frequently found in fairy tales and myths in much the same context as the hero's search for the hard-to-reach treasure, which psychologically means the search for the Self.

2.5.8 The individuation process

An exemplary representation of a unique individuation process based on clinical material and dreams from a personal analysis can be found in Jung's publication *Dream Symbols of the Individuation Process* (CW 12). A further example of a person's individuation process can be found in Jung's work 'The Empiricism of the Individuation Process' (CW 9/1), in which Jung illustrates a woman's individuation process based on a series of pictures painted by her. These pictures also contain examples of mandala symbols. A representation of the unification of opposites as the culminating point of the individuation process can be found in Jung's work *The Psychology of Transference* (CW 16). It is important to emphasise that only a few people go through the individuation process in its deepest form. It represents an archetypal sequence in human life and in principle never comes to its end. Jung emphasised that this process can be thought of as a spiral development, in which an individual encounters the same points again and again in the course of the process, but then processes them at a higher level. The individuation process as a movement towards the totality of the person specifies the direction for the development, but nobody can truly say whether this goal has ever been fully reached.

There is an important difference between the term 'individuality' and that of the 'individuation'. There is certainly a danger that the intense focus on one's own inner life contains a narcissistic and self-concerned element. That is, however, not what Jung means.

> I see it again and again that the individuation process and the realization of consciousness are conflated and therefore the Ego is identified with the Self, which of course forms an incurable confusion of terms. With this Individuation becomes simply egocentrism or autoerotism

[...] Individuation doesn't shut out the world, but rather encompasses it.

(Jung CW 8, p. 432)

On the one hand, individuation means a demarcation, at least in the second half of life, from a complete alignment to external and social demands and standards. As a result, a successful individuation also contains an opposition to the power of archetypal images, which the person does not directly identify themselves with. Much more should be achieved in a conscious conflict with these images, namely the conscious integration of that which truly belongs to one's essence into the personality. This phenomenon would be the opposite of inflation, described above, in which the Ego identifies itself with an archetype and coalesces with it, which usually breaks the personality, since it cannot contain that. 'The purpose of individuation is nothing other than freeing the self from the false shell of the Persona on one hand and the suggestive force of unconscious images on the other' (Jung CW 7, p. 269).

The conception of the individuation process and the midlife crisis was so essential for Jung's psychology that in principle it is possible to formulate a theory of psychopathology based on the individuation process and a stagnation of its development. This was for a long time so essential for analytical psychology that it was explicitly recommended to only conduct Jungian analysis on problems in the second half of life. An exemplary representation of the individuation process in the case of Odysseus can be found in Chapter 5.3.

2.6 Classical works on the core archetypes

Jung himself was concerned extensively with the central archetypes in his work: the mother archetype, the archetype of the (divine) child, the figure of the trickster, the previously mentioned mandalas, and rebirth. These central works will be briefly outlined here.

In his paper 'The Psychological Aspects of the Mother Archetype' (CW 9/1), Jung engages only briefly with the actual archetype of the mother in order to more exhaustively deal with the development and formation of the mother complex which follows. He references at this point his extensive presentation of the mother archetype and how it shaped a young woman's psychotic fantasies in his work *Symbols of Transformation*. The mother archetype can be experienced first-hand in the mother or grandmother, as well as in the stepmother or mother-in-law, or indeed all female nurturing figures. In an impersonal sense the archetype of the mother is embodied in the god mother, the Virgin Mary, Sofia, or the typical polytheistic female gods such as Kybele, Demeter, and so on. Nevertheless the archetype of the mother can also be expressed in abstract images such as of paradise, the (mother) church, the university (alma mater), the city, the country (e.g., Mother Russia), or still more abstractly as the earth, matter, the moon, the cave, and so on. All these forms of expression can be either positive or negative. When positive, the archetype takes the form of the nurturing, protecting, and safety conferring, the supporting (socialisation and teacher) as well as overall the motherly love. The goddesses of destiny, Parzen, as well as the Indian Goddess Kali are, on the other hand, embodiments of the devouring and destructive aspect. Moreover, abstract images like that of the grave, depth, death, or other devouring monsters like Scylla and Charybdis can embody the archetype of the mother. A form of the negative aspect of the mother archetype, which frequently appears in European culture, is the witch or the evil stepmother in fairy tales. Jung's pupil Erich Neumann (1974) has concerned himself much more extensively than even Jung himself with the endless variety of forms of expression of the mother archetype in his comprehensive work (with numerous illustrated representations). He describes in his work a collective process of differentiation, which the archetype of motherliness or femininity can pass through in cultural representations. This might begin, for example, with a figure from earth-like material (chthonian), and extend to the embodiment of the highest form of female intelligence, Sofia. The differentiation in this representation goes clearly far beyond what Jung himself had determined in that it effectively offers a scale of differentiation to be able to organise the different embodiments of the mother archetype.

In his work 'On Rebirth' (CW, 9/1), Jung does something similar for the myth of rebirth, in which he illustrates the different levels or stages of the development of this archetype, for example, identification with a group, identification with cultural heroes, magical processes, and so on. He then exemplifies these different steps using the figure of Chadir, the 'Verdant One', from the eighteenth surah of the Quran, which describes a mystery of rebirth, and goes on to parallel this with numerous cultural and religious examples.

Jung's work on the psychology of the child archetype was originally a part of his collaborative publication with Karl Kerenvi about 'The divine child' (Jung CW, 9/1). Here, Jung illustrated in detail the universal basic structure of the meaning of the 'godly' child. The child begins as something plain and unassuming, born in a plain and improbable place (e.g., Zeus in the cave, Jesus in the stable) and must be hidden from persecution (e.g., from Herod). At the beginning the child is not frequently trusted, although the saviour of his age emerges directly from this unassuming person. Jung went on to prove this basic structure with numerous myths and religious scenes from throughout the world. This is, in my opinion, a hugely successful description of the content and the forms of expression of an archetype because of its structural nature. Moreover, Jung can show here how the motif of the child also emerges, for example, in the dreams of modern clients in psychotherapy. These also contain similar meanings, which can be summarised as 'the child who provides future'. Indeed, the emergence of the motif of the child in psychotherapy is an anticipation of future developments and therefore therapeutically highly meaningful. Typically, the child would initially be denied in dreams, because it appears to be plain and worthless (a typical example for this is the Legend of Christopher, in which the giant initially underestimates the small child's weight beyond all measure). It frequently symbolises, however, precisely the parts and potential of the client out of which the decisive transformation of the personality occurs. Typically, the motif of the child is also the miraculous birth as well as the abandonment and the exposure of the child (see also the motif of the child in the dream series in the case study in Chapter 5.2.3).

Finally, Jung has also extensively covered the figure of the trickster or the rogue ('On the Psychology of the Trickster', Jung CW, 9/1). In European culture this archetypal figure frequently emerges in the form of the fool or *Dümmling*, dumb Hans, or Hanswurst in fairy tales. Jung illustrates in his discourse, however, that this figure has an almost religious meaning and plays an essential role in sacred events in many cultures. The holy clowns in the ceremony of the Pueblo Indians in the Southwestern USA is given as an example. These figures frequently put the finger on painful wounds or taboos in a society, addressing these in the open and set potential healing transformations in motion through this exposure. The trickster is clearly, however, an ambivalent character. He can, through his actions, possess clearly destructive characteristics, but also contains the potential to regard reality impartially or from a new perspective, and by doing so to initiate necessary changes. Similar to the shadow, the trickster will initially be experienced as repulsive and be rejected, but contains unknown value and the potential to alter reality.

2.7 Further classical investigations of archetypes from Jung's successors

It was mentioned above that different basic shapes like the circle (mandala), the cross, the spiral, and the square also represent archetypal carriers of meaning. Ingrid Riedel has worked extensively on these basic shapes and their symbolism (1985a). She (Riedel 1985b) has moreover discussed in her work the symbolism of colours and their archetypal meaning. In a similar way, numbers carry archetypal meaning in them: so, for example, four symbolises totality or a kind of strange ordering (the four seasons, the four cardinal directions, the four evangelists surrounding the figure of Christ, and so on). There are also individual studies devoted to the symbolism of numbers, for example, Betz (1989).

Jung's pupil Marie Louise von Franz (1986) has written on the archetype of eternal youth or *Puer aeternus*. This archetype can be found in the life of people who live, for example, eternally as students, who dodge adult responsibilities and connections, and have problems finding their place in life. An example of this archetype in a cultural narrative is the story of Peter Pan.

Further individual studies can be found on the following archetypes: symbolism of plants (Brosse 1992) and trees (Brosse 1994), of animals (Zerling & Bauer 2003), of the archetype of gardens (Teichert 1986) and of labyrinths (Kern 1999), and of the holy marriage as a connection of masculinity and femininity (Wehr 1998) as well as of the archetype of the fight against the dragon (Steffen 1989). The American Jungian Jean S. Bolen devoted two comprehensive discourses on goddesses (1984) and gods (1989) as personifications of archetypal impacts. The interpretation of gods and heroes from Greek mythology by the New York Jungian Edward Edinger (1994) is also highly recommended. A new complete overview and interpretation of archetypal symbols comes from the Archive of Research in Archetypal Symbolism (ARAS) (2011) at the Jung Institute of Los Angeles. ARAS has made available an excellent website which contains 17,000 depictions of symbols along with numerous articles and discourses about individual symbols, images, and archetypal representations (www.aras.org). An older thorough examination of Jung's immediate students can be found in the anthology *Man and His Symbols* (Jung et al. 1968).

2.8 On the history of the term

Jung was by no means the first to formulate the idea of archetypes. A distinct theory of archetypes, in the sense of principles of organisation in nature, can be found as early as in Johann Wolfgang von Goethe's scientific writings. Similarly, in the wake of Charles Darwin's theory on the evolution of species, the English biologist Richard Owen formulated his own theory of biological archetypes (for an overview, see Hogenson

2001). The historian of psychology Sonu Shamdasani (2003) has illustrated in detail that at the beginning of the twentieth century the idea of archetypes was in the air (see also Lesmeister 2002). Jung knew, for example, the debate in ethnology around Bastian's concept of *Völkergedanken* (peoples' thoughts) (1881). In ethnology, striking similarities in the narrative motifs of ethnic groups living far apart from each other had been apparent for a long time, and from 1880 set into motion a decade-long debate about how this convergence of ideas in fairy tales and myths could be explained (Eisenstädter 1912). Some evidence to illustrate this: in a comparative study of 50 randomly selected cultures, the motif of incest can be found in the mythologies of 39 of these. The majority of the fairy tales found throughout the world can be arranged into just about 100 categories, and for each type examples can be found from completely different parts of the world (Aarne & Thompson 1964). Some examples of universal motifs found in the mythologies of all peoples are the following: the primordial chaos, the separation of the sky and the earth, a devastating flood as a punishment for humanity, the incest of the primordial holy siblings, the theft of fire from the gods.

Two main models of explanation were competing for supremacy at the end of the nineteenth century. The diffusion and transference theory, often called diffusionism, claimed that the reason for the similarities lay in the actual physical contact between peoples in the sense of migration (Eisenstädter 1912). Some authors in this faction went so far as to assume that all peoples on earth stemmed from the same original tribe, the so called 'primal horde', which was supposedly located in an area between the Caucasus and central Asia. Proponents of this theory of physical contact between largely disconnected peoples tried to find evidence for their viewpoint well into the twentieth century. The anthropologist and adventurer Thor Heyerdahl belongs to this group. Based on meticulous archaeological research he reconstructed prehistoric boats and sailed from Egypt to America ('Ra') or from Peru to Easter Island ('Kon Tiki') in order to prove that this physical contact between distant lands was possible in prehistoric times.

The opposing thesis was the theory of elemental thoughts, *Völkergedanken* (Bastian 1881), which stated that the mythological convergence expresses the psychological homogeneity of all people.

> From all sides, from all continents, we encounter in similar conditions a homogenous human thought, an iron necessity of how the plant forms cell ducts or milk vessels depending on the phases of growth, drives out leaves, sets knots, flowers unfold. The fir of the north is different under climatic or local variations, the palm of the tropics is different, but nevertheless the same growth law is present in both.
>
> (p. 14)

It was precisely these thoughts, which were extremely popular in the scientific world in 1900, that Jung incorporated into psychology with his theory of archetypes.

Jung first used the term 'pre-images' in 1912 in his 'Transformations and Symbols of the Libido' (CW 5), and this also signalled the break between Jung and Freud. In this publication, Jung examined the parallels between the fantasy images of a young woman and mythological themes, for example, the myth of the hero. In 1917, Jung described the concept as that of impersonal dominant forces in the psyche which influence behaviour. His first usage of the term archetype appeared in 1919: 'In this deep level we find the a priori, innate forms of intuition, namely the archetypes of perception and cognition, which are the necessary a priori determiners of all mental processes' (Jung 1919, in CW 9/1).

Jung is clearly influenced by Kant's philosophy, which also emphasises that time, space, and causality are a priori forms of apperception ahead of any human perception. In similar ways Jung is also influenced by Plato's idea concept. Jung's pupil Jolande Jacobi (1986) has written on this in her overview of Jungian psychology:

> The archetypal image could be described as self-depiction of the instincts in the psyche, as a picture turned to

a mental process, as a basic pattern of human behaviour. An Aristotelian would say: the archetypes are images formed from the experience of real fathers and mothers. A Platonian would say: the archetypes have first become fathers and mothers because they are pre-images, the prototypes of phenomena. The archetypes are formed a priori for the individual, originating from the collective unconscious and therefore excluded from a sense of individual becoming or fading away.

(p. 51)

In his psychology, in particular in relation to his archetype concept, Jung is an outspoken Platonian. He regards the archetypes as analogues to the Platonic ideas and as preceding every experience. The ideas or respective archetypes first produce the experience of reality by organising the experience of reality.

Jung's experiences with the fantasies of psychiatric patients at the psychiatric clinic at the University of Zurich played a role in forming his concept of archetypes, as well as his study with the association experiment on patients and normal subjects. Jung discovered that the metaphorical language of these psychotic fantasies organised themselves into patterns, which in part paralleled myths and religious metaphors. This material did not come from the memory or experience of his patients – at least that is what Jung assumed (Jung 1968, CW 3). The most important case is that of the 'Solar Phallus Man': a patient in Burghölzli reported that he saw a tube or a phallus coming out of the sun and this made the wind blow. This fantasy coincided strikingly with a mythological picture from an ancient codex. Jung assumed, therefore, that a pre-image must be behind this form of expression and, because the patient had no knowledge whatsoever of this ancient myth, the picture could not have been gained through experience and must be inherent (see also Blair 2003, Shamadasani 2003).

In his 'Association Studies' (CW 2), Jung researched under experimental conditions the reactions of test subjects to certain emotionally meaningful terms and was able to show that in the human unconscious there are affectively charged and semi-autonomous factors, the complexes. Along with this, it became apparent to him that there were a series of complexes which were present in many test subjects and which were interindividually similar, in their emotional contents, and in the images and experiences (e.g., the negative mother complex). The coinciding core of these complexes was what Jung described as the pre-image of the archetype.

In 1947, Jung made a distinction between the archetype, which is not accessible, and the archetypal image, its concrete expression, which can be experienced subjectively. The archetype is a form without content, comparable with the structure of crystal, which leads to the formation of a concrete crystal in a solution. The concrete crystal is different each time, but the general structural arrangement of the molecules is the same in all crystals. Jung similarly assumed that the concrete contents of the archetypal expressions were conditioned by cultural influences.

2.9 Parallel concepts in general psychoanalysis

As has already been previously mentioned, Jung's formulation of his archetype concept led to his break with Freud. It would be expected, therefore, that there must be a fundamental difference between the Freudian and Jungian tradition. Concepts like the archetype, however, are not unknown in psychoanalysis in the sense of the Freudian tradition. Freud had already described a limited number of so-called pre-fantasies, of which the so-called pre-scenes are the most meaningful. Freud assumed that, before any experience, the child brings with them all inner images and fantasies related to, for example, sexual union of the parents. The British psychoanalyst Melanie Klein expanded this assumption and conjectured that a whole system of archaic images existed in infants, for example, the image of a mother who devours the infant (Klein 1957). These images would be particularly significant for the development of psychopathologies. The Freudian tradition does not, like the Jungian tradition, assume that these archaic images have a healing effect in the therapeutic process, but rather the opposite, that they can lead to developmental disturbances in children if they are stimulated. Nevertheless, there was intense cooperation between the British Jungians and the British school of Object Relations Theory, which Melanie Klein was a part of, because of these seemingly related concepts (e.g., between the British psychoanalyst Donald Winnicott and the British Jungian Michael Fordham). This cooperation shaped the development of the British school of analytical psychology, often referred to as the developmental school (Samuels 1986.

In current concepts of psychodynamic therapy, there appears to be a fundamental convergence of traditions. Modern psycho-dynamic therapies assume that all children bring with them a set of basic needs (e.g., the need for attachment), and healthy development depends on whether these basic needs are met or nurtured. Attachment theory represents an important bridge between the traditions and indeed even seems to offer a new basic theory of all psychodynamic approaches (Rudolf 2000). The Jungian Anthony Stevens (2003) on the other hand sees in the universal need for attachment empirical evidence for Jung's archetypes.

2.10 Parallels to the collective unconscious in other schools of psychotherapy

Freud observed in his structural theory that the individual psyche 'contains traces of memories from the experiences of earlier generations' (Freud 1939, p. 546). Meanwhile, in the Freudian tradition, there are different concepts which come very close to the concept of a collective unconscious, at least when it is defined as an unconscious that different people share with each other (e.g., in a family). The concept of an inter-personal unconscious, as it is formulated by the American psychoanalysts and couple therapists Sharff and Sharff (2014), also bears some similarity:

> In the overall picture, we come to the realization that we live in an unconscious sphere. Each of us carries his own part of this, each of us obtains structure and enrichment

through this. Our own unconscious and affective life is made up of many different components. It is a mix of that which is innate and the situation we were born into, as well as the interactions we have with the people we meet in the course of our life cycle – with parents, siblings, extended family, teachers, friends, colleagues, and finally the larger social and cultural environment. The unconscious is not individual, as Freud assumed: it is in a fundamental sense interpersonal, while we have likewise the feeling that it quintessentially belongs to us. We are social creatures, not only in what affects our behaviour and interactions, rather up to the deepest levels of out spirit and psyche [...] The dynamic unconscious is in every respect interpersonal. It forms in this way an interpersonal matrix. It is constructed from a dynamic system of inner relationships and manifests itself in personal decisions, behaviour, and relationships. Today, we cannot regard the unconscious, and accordingly the topographic model of the human psyche or the structure theory as they were originally conceptualised by Freud, as exclusively belonging to the individual. Although my unconscious is unique and belongs only to me, we share it also with our closest life-partner, our work colleagues, and other social units, with whom we are in reciprocal relationships. The unconscious develops in dynamic interaction with the unconscious sphere in which it finds itself. The sphere is constituted from shared unconscious presuppositions in the family and society or the repressed or ignored aspects of social life, the culture and history, the values and the family relationships, into which we are born. Children are born into all that which previous generations have suffered and repressed.

(Scharff & Sharff 2014, p. 18ff)

It sounds almost as if Jung had written it himself.

The terms interpersonal unconscious, the sphere, and the link (as they can be found in the psychoanalytic theories of Dicks, Baranger and Willi) as well as the concept of an unconscious in the psychoanalytic couple and family therapy can also be considered as related to the idea of a collective unconscious; in particular in couple therapy, the concept of a couple relationship emerging from a shared unconscious with shared fantasies as well as an unconscious dynamic, for which in German-speaking countries the term *Kollusion* has been used, developed some time ago (for extensive coverage of this, see Scharff & Sharff 2014). This is very similar to the concept of the social unconscious, by which the mental representation of the power of history and culture and their influence on the individual is meant. This is very closely related to the concept of the cultural complex as Singer (Singer & Kimbles 2004) conceives it (see Chapter 6).

Furthermore, although he was always extremely sceptical of Jung's parapsychological interests, Freud dealt with phenomena of an unconscious transference under the heading of telepathy, as the following passage shows:

> As is well known, no-one knows how the collective will in the large insect states comes into being. Possibly it happens due to such direct mental transference. We can conjecture, that this is the original, archaic route to understanding amongst individuals, which in the course of phylogenetic development has been repressed through better methods of communication with help from signals which can be comprehended by the senses. But the old method could remain in the background and could still assert itself under certain conditions, for example in passionately excited crowds.
>
> (Freud 1933, p. 59f)

Later, the psychoanalyst Rene Spitz (1965), who in the 1950s and 1960s dealt with the early relationship between mother and child, shaped the term 'co-anaesthetic' perception. What is meant by this term is that the infant, which truly only has a few available modes of communication with their caregiver, is in contact with the mother via different non-verbal sensory channels, such as skin contact, smell, the sense of muscle tension, and in this way can convey relatively complex information about its current condition to the mother. To a somewhat limited extent this also happens on the part of the mother to her child. Spitz assumes that even for a small child this sensory perception regresses with time and is replaced or overtaken by other, particularly verbal, communication channels, but that the basic human ability for such a form of interaction never fully vanishes. Other psychoanalysts formed in the wake of Spitz's work the notion of the 'sphere' for this exchange process (Gödde & Buchholz 2011). The psychoanalysts Günter Gödde and Michael Buchholz (2011) have recently edited an overview of writings on this phenomenon and the related concepts.

But these phenomena had not only awoken interest and attempts at conceptualisation in the field of psychoanalysis. In systemic family therapy, the principle of delegation was described by Helm Stierlin, in which parents unconsciously give orders to their children that in some ways completely shape the children's life experience and value systems. The children thus live out their parents' unaccomplished tasks or desires. While doing so they pursue systematically and with huge amounts of effort, complex careers, without being able to specify when asked why they are really doing this. These concepts are summarised in current family therapy under the term 'transgenerational' perspectives, although it must be said that these thoughts originally go back to the psychoanalyst Horst Eberhard Richter. It is assumed here that a transmission of family patterns and issues (e.g., alcoholism, violence) spanning several generations exists which is closely intertwined with individual pathologies. Along with this comes the interesting question of how such complex behavioural patterns are transmitted from generation to generation, in particular in cases where children have practically no contact with the troubled parents in question. These phenomena and processes of passing on have received particular attention and been the subject of scientific research in the area of transgenerational transmission of psychotrauma, especially with relation to families of Holocaust survivors (for an overview, see Rauwald 2013). Symptoms that highly resemble those of post-traumatic stress can be seen in second- and third-generation family members of survivors of the Shoah, in Israel in particular. This afflicts children and grandchildren of the victims who show no visible evidence of trauma. The more strongly the first generation were traumatised and the less they have talked about this with their descendants, the more pronounced the phenomenon is in the later generations. Even though the phenomenon has been systematically observed and described in a number countries and in other groups, the question of how this information about the experiences of a generation is transmitted to other generations has not been conclusively answered. Research into attachment provides at least some insight here, as it has been observed that traumatised mothers transfer specific emotions to their child through mimicry and other channels, and through this develop in their child an emotional condition similar to their own (Cassidy & Shaver 2018.

In the so-called *Aufstellungsarbeit* (family reconstruction) methods used in family therapy, it has long been claimed that when a constellation of a family structure is acted out with the aid of role players, a patient confers to these actors unconscious knowledge about themselves. The role players can feel, for example, body language which originates with the family members of the patient (the 'field of knowledge' in the family constellation). This method was recently investigated in a randomised controlled study as part of a series of studies conducted for the Sonderforschungsbereich 619 (special research area of the German Research Association) 'Ritual Dynamics' at the University of Heidelberg (Jungaberle et al. 2006). A sample of 208 adult participants were assigned randomly either to an experimental group with a three-day family reconstruction workshop or to a waiting list control group. The effectiveness of the intervention was judged initially after two weeks and then again four months after the workshop with standardised measures used in psychotherapy. The results prove clearly the effectiveness of this approach regarding measures of mental health. This applies also for the participants in the experimental group, who only observed the work and acted as representatives of family members. These results potentially serve as proof for the existence of the claimed unconscious transfer effects in the reconstruction work. Nevertheless, the aim of the experiment was not to explore the claim of an unconscious transfer from family members to role players.

3 Criticism of the classic concept of the archetype and expansions

Even at the early stages of the formulation of the archetype concept, Jung was heavily criticised. This came above all from Freud and his direct proponents, which as is well known also led to a decade-long estrangement between the two analytical schools. Jung faced attacks because of his archetype concept from academic psychology and the humanities as well. The general accusations, even up to the present day, are essentially as follows: the concept is mystifying and obfuscating, rather than illuminating anything; the location of the origins of the archetypes in a transcendental sphere takes it beyond the boundaries of normal science and the concept is, as a result, no longer empirically provable; finally, Jung comes close to an ultimately fascistic mindset with his concept of archetypes, something not helped by his problematic remarks in the time of National Socialism.

From my perspective, the concept of archetypes seems to be controversial. While some points of criticism are clearly justified, others are easily refuted. For me, it seems as though Jung, contrary to his otherwise rather open and less dogmatic attitude towards scientific questions, was especially emotionally involved with his archetype concept. He, therefore, vehemently, and even at times defiantly, defended his concept against well-intentioned and entitled criticism. A good example of this is the criticism of the biologist Adolf Portmann, with whom Jung had close contact at the Eranos conferences. Portmann indicated that Jung's assertion that archetypes are the deposit of humanity's

DOI: 10.4324/9781003058458-3

experiences throughout the entirety of history is, from an evolutionary perspective, similar to the position of Lamarckism; this has long been refuted because individual experience is not transmitted genetically. Instead of considering Portmann's objection, however, Jung reviled Portmann behind his back and even accused him of not having understood the archetype concept. Considering both the level of knowledge at the time and from today's perspective, however, Portmann was completely correct. Jung even recognised this himself at some point, and in 1947 corrected his archetype concept with consideration of Portmann's objection, although he did not mention Portmann (see also Shamadasani 2003 for extensive coverage).

3.1 Problems and contradictions in the Jungian concept of archetypes

In the case of the Solar Phallus man, just as in the other cases described early on by Jung, there was the fundamental problem of proving that no kind of cryptomnesia had taken place, that the affected person had not somehow in the past come into contact with the mythological contact and now unconsciously remembered it. If the archetype is to be defined as inherent, it cannot be gained from enculturation. To prove this in a specific case, however, is very difficult and Jung's assumption, therefore, stands frequently on shaky ground (see also Bair 2003).

Raya Jones (2007) has also made an interesting argument against the solar phallus case and similar cases as evidence for the existence of archetypes: if there really were an archetype behind the fantasy of the solar phallus, this fantasy would have to be exhibited far more frequently than just from one single patient as well as in a single old codex. Even Jung himself demonstrated in the archetype concept inconsistencies and contradictions, which have already been referenced many times (see e.g., Hogenson 2004, Saunders & Skar 2001, Samuels 1986). If Jung's writings on the term archetype are subjected to a critical analysis, then at least four different types of definitions can be found. Jung's concept of archetypes is an attempt to bring together perspectives of traditional science with thoughts which go beyond the narrow definitions of science. This is a principle topic that permeates Jung's scientific work, which can also be seen in his decade-long discourse with the Nobel Prize-winning physicist Wolfgang Pauli on the theory of synchronicity (see Atmanspacher 1995). For the archetype concept, however, what emerged from this was a certain multiplicity, indeed a contradictoriness, which Jung could not unite into a truly coherent definition throughout his life (for an extensive discussion of this related problem, see Roesler 2012b). It is clear, though, that a major aspect of Jung's works is to incorporate concepts from the natural sciences without giving up a transcendental perspective. The different aspects of his attempts at definition are illustrated in the following section as well as their after-effects in analytical psychology to the present day, because these various aspects have partially shaped the development of individual schools within analytical psychology.

3.1.1 Biological definition

Jung argued again and again, and maintained this until the end of his life, that archetypes are transmitted via biological pathways, that is, genetically (even though he did not use the term), like instincts in animals:

> this term does not relate to an inherited experience, but rather presuppositions of experience, an inherited mode of mental functioning, corresponding to inherent ways in which the chicken hatches an egg, the bird builds its nest, a certain type of wasp strings the motor ganglion of a grub, and eels find their way to Bermuda and so on [...] in other words, it is a pattern of behaviour. This aspect of the archetype, the completely biological aspect, is the only object of scientific psychology.
>
> (Jung CW 18, p. 1228)

As far back as Jung and from other representatives of this direction of analytical psychology, parallels are drawn to ethology and the concept of the innate release mechanism (see Tinbergen

1978). In the development of his archetype concept, Jung was apparently strongly influenced by the then newly emerging behavioural science in biology and borrowed explicitly from this, for example, with the concept of the *pattern of behaviour*.

The main representative of this position today among Jungians, who has taken this concept further with the inclusion of newer findings from, for example, attachment research, is Anthony Stevens (Stevens & Price 1996): 'Archetypes are understood as neuro-psychic units, which are formed through natural selection and which are responsible for the determination of behavioural characteristics as well as for the typical human emotions and cognitive experiences' (p. 6). This school of thought can be described as evolutionary psychology or psychiatry.

3.1.2 Empirical statistical definition

In his association studies Jung achieved the following empirical observations: a) there are unconscious thematic complexes which centre around a thematic centre, and b) empirically a large number of individuals' complexes fall into a limited number of categories; therefore, there are among a large number of investigated individuals only a limited number of continually repeated fundamental themes. Jung's hypothesis here is: at the heart of these categories there is an archetype, which directs the life of the individual and brings out their interindividual homogeneity. This line of argument was taken up recently by Saunders and Skarr (2001), who developed a mathematical definition of the archetype and claimed that archetypes are the complexes which fall statistically into the same categories.

3.1.3 Transcendental definition

In contrast to his frequently biologically oriented argument, Jung also expressed again and again that archetypes stem from a transcendental level; they are ubiquitous and are present in all human experience; and they are not representable or accessible to conscious experience and have no physical place. In

1947, Jung wrote about the archetype: 'The true nature of the archetype is not consciously apprehendable, that means it is transcendent, therefore I call it psychoid'. He points out the parallels to Plato's idea concept: 'the eternal ideas are primordial images, which are stored in an otherworldly place as transcendent forms' (Jung CW 9/1, p. 68). Jung confers to the archetype, moreover, almost otherworldly qualities: 'the archetype determines the type and the process of the shaping with apparent pre-knowledge or in *a priori* possession of the goal' (Jung CW 8, p. 411). His thoughts on the psychoid unconscious present a thesis on the question of the connection between spirit and matter. It was with this aspect of Jung's theory that conventional science, in the sense of 'normal science', always had enormous problems. Jung must be given credit here for his attempts to create a theoretical connection between spirit and matter. Not only his exchange with the nuclear physicist Pauli, but also different current theories and experiments in the world of quantum physics, make it clear that Jung's theses were in no way unscientific nonsense (Roesler 2013, 2015). Towards the end of his life, Jung reflected on a notion of a psychoid unconscious, which had emerged out of the decade-long discourse with the quantum physician Pauli, also known as 'Unus Mundus theory'. Starting from insights about the physical laws of the quantum world, Jung postulated that the (collective) unconscious represented analogously an area of potential, which is structured through the archetypes as imperceptible and not directly experienceable organisers. Only when these cross over the threshold into perceptible reality do they decide if they manifest themselves as bodily material or as mental spirit (for an extensive discussion and further development of this, see Atmanspacher 1995, 2014; Atmanspacher et al. 2002, 2013. The perception that the archetypes stem from a transcendental level, to which all humans have access, was taken further, most prominently by James Hillman in his 'archetypal psychology' (Hillman 1983). Here the question is not where the archetypes come from, but rather what their effects as shaping forces are: 'Archetypal psychology begins neither in the physiology of the brain, the structure of language, the organisation of society, nor in the analysis of behaviour, but rather in the processes of the imagination' (Hillman 1983, p. 19).

3.1.4 Cultural psychological behaviour

After his reformulation of archetype theory in 1947 and the distinction between the archetype per se and its concrete manifestations, Jung said clearly that the concrete form of the archetype and its contents were contingent on cultural factors (Jung CW 9/1, p. 67). Above all, however, a cultural psychological approach to the archetype can be found in the way that Jung was concerned with mythology, fairy tales, and religious stories. Here Jung proceeds clearly in a hermeneutic way and deals with the archetypal images as expressions of culture, which can only be investigated through interpretation. Prominent here is particularly his work on alchemy as well as on religious symbols and rituals, such as, for example, the consecration in the Catholic mass and on mandalas.

What is problematic is that Jung, despite this practically hermeneutic direction, at the same time insisted that archetypes are genetically transmitted. Jung finds himself here in a tradition of German philosophy from Baruch de Spinoza and Gottfried Wilhelm Leibniz, to Immanuel Kant, and up to its modern form in the 'Philosophy of Symbolic Forms' (Cassirer 1955). This line of argument sees humans as animal symbolism, which means that the human approach to reality is structured by the forms inherent in the human mind. Jung here explicitly refers to Kant. Jung himself spoke persistently about the fact that archetypes shape perception and imagination. Pietikainen (1998) has expanded this line of thought in Jung's works: the human mind possesses in itself universal forms, which transform the impressions and perceptions from the world into symbols and, by the connection of symbols, into different cultural forms such as language, myth, art, and so on. These universal forms are in a way anchored in the structure of the human mind. Our perception of the world and our 'world understanding' are not only given to us through the shape of external data, but also are formed by being subjected to a process of linguistic, mythical, or logical-theoretical apperception in the human mind. Only what results from this process exists for us psychologically. In this process universal forms manifest themselves, what could be equated with Jung's idea of archetypes.

In the distinctive juxtaposition of these four views of the archetype, all coming from Jung, it becomes clear that these conceptualisations in part contradict one another. In any case, Jung never offered a consistent theory. Jung appears to mix together the different definitions: when he, for example, advocates for the transcendental understanding of archetypes, he insists simultaneously that archetypes are transmitted biologically and genetically. In addition, the later concept of the archetype per se, as only a form and free of content, was hardly maintained by Jung. Instead, numerous examples of archetypes according to Jung are determined very clearly by their content (e.g., the archetype of the hero myth).

A further central problem of the archetype concept as formulated by Jung is that very different entities are described as archetypal. To name but a few:

- Primitive modes of perception (e.g., being held)
- Creatures and objects (e.g., the archetype of the snake)
- Social patterns and rules (e.g., marriage)
- Narrative patterns (e.g., the myth of the hero)
- Images and shapes (e.g., the cross)
- Rituals (e.g., initiation)
- Religious ideas (e.g., the sacrifice)

Up to the present day, no systematisation or theoretical clarification has taken place in analytical psychology related to the question of what exactly is meant by the term archetype. There is also continuing confusion in the debate as to what purpose the term should actually serve, how it is benefiting our understanding, and what the clinical use of the concept is – it has be noted that in analytical psychology, archetype theory is used as a psychotherapeutic approach. From my perspective, the archetype concept fulfils above all two functions in analytical psychology. On the one hand, it is a cultural theory, therefore one approach to explaining the remarkable intercultural convergence in religious and mythological ideas in images patterns, rituals, and so on. On the other hand, as part of a psychotherapeutic approach, here is a clinical use of the concept: in crisis situations or with mental disturbances the universally present archetypes, which are expressed in dreams and symbolic material, structure or trigger the healing process in the individual psyche. This process is supported by the therapeutic framework and the relationship (see Chapter 5).

An example which illustrates this understanding can be found in the so-called Tavistock lectures, which Jung gave at the Tavistock Clinic in London in 1935 and that served as an introduction to his psychology at the time (Jung CW 18). In the third lecture Jung explicitly deals with the therapeutic application of archetypal elements in a dream. Jung is concerned here with the dream of a 40-year-old man with symptoms of vertigo. In the man's dream, a monster appears in the form of a crab. Jung interprets this symbol as a message from the unconscious that the cerebral spine and sympathetic nervous system of the dreamer are rebelling against the patient's conscious mindset, because a crab only has this form of a nervous system. Here, a common practice in both Jung and modern-day analytical psychology becomes clear. The idea is that the client's unconscious produces in the archetypal symbol a connection to a body of knowledge that is not accessible to the consciousness of the dreamer. In this way, the archetypal element confers an additional piece of information, which transcends consciousness and that is aimed at healing the patient and can be made useful in the therapeutic process. This information comes from an area outside of consciousness and also was, by definition, never conscious and never a part of the person's experience. A huge number of examples of this understanding and this practice can be found in analytical psychology, for example, in the use of fairy tales and other mythological narratives. Thus, a dream resembles a mythological narrative and this delivers information about the further necessary development of the personality, the therapy, and so on (see Chapter 5.3).

Here the deciding question for a discussion on the term archetype emerges, namely where this information comes from if it had never been experienced by the dreamer. It will be clear here, that the Jungian therapist places faith in the fact that all of the archetypal information for every client is potentially accessible and under the given conditions is activated and can be 'constellated'. This means that analytical psychology must assume without question the universality of archetypes. On the other hand, it makes clear that archetypes deal with complex symbolic information, namely process patterns, which describe the development from a starting point to a solution and that can, therefore, be conceived of in narrative form.

Criticism of the Anima/Animus concept and the resulting extensions of this theory have already been referred to above (Chapter 2.5.5). The foremost criticism is that patriarchally biased clichéd roles, as were typical for Jung's time, are expressed in both concepts. This is not reflected by Jung, however, as he cements these clichéd roles as general and independent of time. James Hillman, a direct pupil of Jung, has referred primarily in his criticism to the confusion of terms and the unclear distinction of definitions in the term Anima and thereby clarified contradictions in Jung's conception (Hillman 1981a, 1981b). Hillman differentiates more clearly than Jung between the Anima and the Eros principle, as well as between the Anima and emotion and defines femininity more clearly from this concept.

In the 1980s, a more fundamental critique of the whole concept of the soul image began, formulated primarily by Verena Kast and Ursula Baumgart (for a comprehensive discussion, see Heisig 1996). Baumgardt (1987) in particular criticised in her book *King Drosselbart and C. J. Jung's Image of Women: Critical Thoughts on the Anima and Animus* how heavily dependent Jung's image of women was on the contemporary zeitgeist and illustrated how he inhibited with this a real understanding of the feminine psyche. Alongside the aforementioned criticism of Jung's use of patriarchal clichés (why should Logos be reserved for the man and Eros for the woman?), the core of Kast's argument (1979) is that in modernity, men as well as women each live with masculine as well as feminine characteristics and orientations, and therefore a fundamental problem appears with the concept of the gendered soul image. For Kast, taking this into account would require both archetypes in both genders to be considered (Kast 1984). This makes possible on the one hand a differentiated description and demarcation for the qualities connected both with the Anima and the Animus, and on the other hand a differentiated consideration for a specific person of their whole mental situation, independent of which masculine or feminine qualities they consciously live and that, following the principle of opposition, can be regarded as unconscious parts. In this sense, the therapeutic work with these inner figures can also help provide a definitive detachment from the masculine and feminine images of parents.

For all these authors, moreover, one fundamental problem is visible in Jung's psychology, namely his insistence on a theory of polarity and the absolute applicability of the principle of opposites for all archetypes. It is precisely this, particularly related to the Anima/Animus concept, that brings Jung into theoretical difficulty and causes problems for his definition. In the overview of the criticism presented here, it stands to reason for me to suggest a clear separation of the archetypes discussed here from descriptions of the behaviour and experience of actual men and women. For me, one of the basic problems here appears to lie in Jung's formulation of the concept because, on the one hand, he takes trouble over an objective description of masculine and feminine mentality and, on the other hand, orients this around the concrete behaviour of real men and women, which is also necessarily contingent on a time. From other authors, for example, Schwartz-Salant, it has therefore been suggested that instead of the terms masculine and feminine, we rather use unloaded formulations for these abstract principles, for example, Sol and Luna, which seems to me to be extremely reasonable.

It must generally be understood that inside of analytical psychology, criticism from other areas of science is hardly perceived and there is little debate in particular in relation to the concept of the archetype. An example of this kind of criticism, which is argued soundly throughout, can be found, for example, in Petzold et al. (2014):

> This assertion of the culturally overlapping meaning of archetypes must, therefore, also be critically considered. C. G. Jung assumes a collective unconscious of the human species, but it is based rather on culturally determined interiorised collectivities, for which Moscovici's socio-psychological conception of a 'collective mental presentation' – conscious, preconscious, unconscious mentalisations – offers an alternative for the explanation of myth forming structural elements (archetypes).
>
> (p. 439f)

Subsequently, the authors give numerous examples of the same elements or symbols in various cultures having completely different meanings based on geographical or climate conditions. For example, in the north the sun contains a warmth-giving motherly power, while in desert areas it contains a threatening character and is assigned to the area of evil. It is argued further:

> The assumption of, as it were, genetically predisposed mythologems and archetypes of heroes and goddesses even comes into the realm of mythotropic conceptualization. What is powerful in archetypes, myths, and symbols must be current in the collective mental representation and passed down in a process of socio-historical transmission, otherwise it is not present. The attempt by Kerenyi, together with C. G. Jung, to see the figures of Greek mythology as pre-images of the human soul must, in addition to the criticism that it takes too little account of the socio-historical and socio-economic conditions of the ancient world or that it does not seek to create a connection between explanations in terms of mental history, counter the Eurocentrism associated with recourse to antiquity.
>
> (p. 441)

The sophisticated arguments of Norbert Bischof (1996), who is intensely concerned with Neumann's continuation of Jung's archetype theory in his work *The History and Origins of Consciousness* (see Chapter 3.2.2), have a similar target to the above criticism, namely the way in which alternative explanatory concepts were not considered enough by Jung as well as by his successors. Bischoff argues that the conformity in the myths of different peoples can be understood as a reflection of general human experience, especially in ontogeny, and that no kind of genetic or other preformed predisposition need be assumed for them to exist. Moreover, Bischoff accuses Neumann in particular of having discarded certain myths which did not fit with the concept of his argument. It is astounding that practically no engagement with these arguments can be found in Jungian literature and how overall the theoretical debate in analytical psychology shows itself to be closed off to other schools of theory and science as well as a lack of self-reflective criticism.

The justification of the criticism mentioned above as well as the level of knowledge about the validity of the concept of archetypes will be assessed after the detailed description of the state of research on the concept (Chapter 4.2.7).

3.2 Expansions of the archetype concept from Jung's direct pupils

3.2.1 Michael Fordham's theory of the process of deintegration and reintegration as an extension of Jung's theory of the Self

One of Jung's pupils in London, Michael Fordham, who was in close contact with the Freudian psychoanalysts in Great Britain, in particularly the founders of the psychoanalytic object-relations theory, Melanie Klein, Donald Winnicott, and others, expanded in his own theories the Jungian concept of the Self and attempted to include elements of developmental psychology. The British school of psychoanalysis had laid the foundations for a psychoanalysis of childhood and was therefore concerned with issues of developmental psychology.

> Jung's theories of the Self were expanded later to a developmental psychological concept. As part of this concept it was postulated that a primal or original Self already exists at the beginning of life. This primal Self contains all inherent, archetypal potential which can be expressed in a person. In a suitable environment this potential begins, in a process of deintegration, to develop out from the original state, which is integrated with the unconscious, by seeking equivalents in the outside world. The emerging 'pairing' of the active archetypal potential of the child with the re-active answer of the mother is then reintegrated and becomes an internalised object. This process of deintegration and reintegration repeats itself throughout life [...] gradually the fragments of the Ego present in the deintegrated pieces come together to form the Ego. The primal Self is assigned a defence system which is most pronouncedly activate in situations in which, from the point of view of the child, the environment has been insufficient.
>
> (Samuels et al. 1986, p. 200f)

3.2.2 *Erich Neumann's* History and Origins of Consciousness

Erich Neumann, who was born in 1905 in Berlin and later immigrated to Israel, where he laid the foundations for an analytical community, surely belongs to Jung's most significant direct pupils and colleagues. Apart from the publication mentioned above, Neumann became known primarily for his comprehensive representation of the symbolism of the archetype of the mother, the feminine psychology, and his work on the connection between depth psychology and ethics. In his *History and Origins of Consciousness* (1968), Neumann undertook the task of interpreting all the world's existing myths and fairy tales along one central line, a kind of strand of development of archetypal themes. The central theme of this development is the developing and increasing emancipation of the conscious Ego, that appears in the figure of the masculine hero, out of the unconscious, which appears in the figure of the controlling, clutching, devouring form of the mother. Through this, Neumann develops a cultural history of myths, whose beginning he locates in the Stone Age cultures of the great mother goddess, the animal mistress. The later agricultural societies of the Neolithic era also worship still fertile femininity in the mystery of the germination and growth of plants from the seeds, which these societies depended on for their existence. Only slowly in the myths does a nascent masculine consciousness appear, one that wants to detach itself from the mother goddess, which is being contained in the unconscious, and increasingly emancipate itself. This struggle for release from the control of the (feminine) unconscious is described to us in well-known hero myths, which will be more comprehensively dealt with below. The comprehensive interpretation of the Odyssey conducted later presents in principle a depth psychological reading, oriented closely around Neumann, of such a prototypical hero myth.

Neumann's representation, which in its coherence and consistency is very convincing, enjoys great respect within the world of analytical psychology. It is surprisingly rarely acknowledged, however, that Neumann's conception was in ethnology as well as psychology clearly criticised and, in my opinion, also convincingly refuted. Bischof (1996) can, for example, convincingly prove that the choice of myths investigated by Neumann was highly selective, that Neumann pointedly dismissed and disregarded those myths which did not fit with his interpretation. By contrast, Bischof presents an alternative concept that describes the psychological meaning of the myths from the experience of man in its ontogenetic development.

3.2.3 *The archetypal psychology of James Hillman*

James Hillman's so-called archetypal psychology represents perhaps the most consistent and at the same time the most extreme continuation of Jung's archetype concept. Hillman was a direct pupil of Jung and for many years was the director of studies at the Jung Institute in Zürich. This means he also had a substantial influence on the development and formation of the education of psychotherapists in the Jungian school. After a sexual relationship with an analysand led to a scandal at the Jung Institute, Hillman left the institute in Zürich and operated from then on in the USA, mostly at the Jung Institute in Los Angeles.

The so-called archetypal psychology expands on Jung's understanding of archetypes, but is rather such a subtle and complex further development, which likewise stands in open confrontation to usual forms of Western thinking, that it is extremely difficult in the scope of this book to give a brief overview of it. Many of its arguments sound as if they could almost be approaching ideas and practices from the New Age, esotericism, and the like. That would be, however, a fundamental misunderstanding. Archetypal psychology is instead based on profound philosophical and anthropological considerations. These can only be, however, briefly unpicked here, and so it must be prefaced by saying that here some things will also appear to be misleading. The basic idea for Hillman is that the archetypes, as experienceable images, present in general the fundamental reality and they are prior to not only every subjectivity but also before reality in general (e.g., Hillman 1979). This is, in principle, a radical continuance of Jung's concept of the 'objective psyche'. The human capacity for imagination is their access to this antecedent reality of images. As stated, imagination is here understood as more than a subjective experience, in which subjective inner worlds are created by the mind. Imagination is rather a mode of perception, which makes it possible for us to access the actual reality of images. This perception also has the consequence that images are no longer interrogated about a subjective reality lying behind, but instead it is about the subject opening itself to these images, an idea which is also transferred to analytical therapy. Essentially, at the heart of the matter is the question of how we relate to these always prior existing images. Hillman even emphasises that our conventional terms of reality and fantasy could exchange places. In the same way, mythology according to Hillman experiences a dramatic appreciation of value, it is 'the primal and unreproducible language of the archetypal pattern, the metaphorical discourse of myth' (1983, p. 2). Jung already understood the gods of ancient mythology as the personification of the inner psyche and ultimately archetypal qualities, although for Jung this approach remained relative and metaphorical. For Hillman it experiences a radical elevation, aptly summarised by Hillman's pupil Miller:

> The gods and goddesses are signs of forces and powers which possess autonomy and are not determined or influenced by social and historical events, not by wills or the arguments of humans, not by personal or individual factors. They make themselves felt as influencing agents that give shape to social, intellectual, and personal behaviour.
>
> (quoted in Samuels, 1986, p. 424)

Ultimately, therefore, the archetypes and their forms of appearance in images and personifications are no longer located in an inner soul and ultimately subject-relative sphere, but they are rather accepted as the ultimate reality before any subjectivity. The logical consequence in the archetypal psychological school is the development of a modern, so-called psychological polytheism, in which the gods of Greek antiquity in particular will be revitalised as essential reference values for psychology. This perspective has, of course, famous predecessors in the European Renaissance, and Hillman and his pupils also refer sequentially to a line of philosophers from this time period, namely Marsilio Ficino and Giovanni Battista Vico. For Ficino, for instance, there is a trichotomous model of the psyche, where the mind or rational intellect is in the first position, in the second comes the imagination or fantasy, and in the third position we find the body or nature. In the same way, a special emphasis or appreciation of the imagination can be found in Vico's thoughts, and he speaks of universal images as we encounter them in myths. For Vico, the 12 gods of Olympus represent fundamental structures. More strikingly even than for Hillman himself, for some of his pupils this has indeed had very fruitful consequences. Thomas Moore (1996) particularly should be mentioned here, as he has achieved enormous popularity in the USA with his publications and has for years partly led the bestseller list. Archetypal psychology has also had an enormous influence on the men's movement and the formation of a male psychology, and has led to practical applications in work with men's groups. Robert Bly (1990), one of Hillman's pupils, has illustrated in his work *Iron John*, with reference to the fairy tale of the same name from the collection of the Brothers Grimm, the archetypal way to a masculine identity. Two of his pupils, Robert Moore and Douglas Gillette (1991), have consequently developed an applied concept of four archetypes, which constitute masculinity: king, warrior, magician, and lover. As an example of a current application, a psychotherapeutic self-experience-oriented men's group was developed on the basis of various archetypes that make up masculinity (see Chapter 5.2.7). Richard Rohr (1996) also finds that the concept of archetypes of masculinity applies for the revitalisation of Christian spiritual*ity*. The implication for the subject of this approach to archetypal psychology leads to the formation of a new concept of 'spirit'. Spirit is essentially in this sense the place in which the experience of the archetypal images and deities becomes possible, although it is no longer merely a part of the inner spirit, a part of the personality so to speak, but rather an interstice which is not only subjective.

> But spirit is ultimately also a mode of being and perception as well as an actuality. Seen in this way, the spirit needs the human for its incarnation just as much as the human ultimately needs the spirit. It follows then that analysis doesn't entail healing the spirit, but rather supporting the spirit – it isn't concerned with the deep-seated problems, but rather with letting the problems become more deeply rooted.
>
> (Samuels 1986, p. 429)

Healing occurs in psychotherapy, therefore, not through images being highlighted, worked through, and finally integrated into the personal psyche, but rather that the personal psyche opens up for the prior reality of the images and essentially submits to them. Hillman emphasises, for example, that the Ego should not be strengthened but rather be weakened. Dreams are a reality that exists outside of us, which calls on us (Hillman 1979). Ultimately it is about 'growing down'.

Archetypal psychology also has, of course, a therapeutic practice. Indeed, this is experiencing a reconceptualisation: 'Ultimately analysis is also a form of enactment of an archetypal fantasy' (Hillman 1975, p. 128). Archetypal psychology strives for the 'entry into the larger radius of the imaginative tradition of the West, that leaves the consulting room behind' (Hillman 1983, p. 1). The general line in practice is in principle a relativisation of the Ego and places great emphasis on the role of the shadow as that which is marginalised or even rejected by the subjective, rational intellect (Hillman 1979). At the centre of this is naturally the engagement with images and how they emerge, for example, in the dreams of patients. Hillman strongly emphasised that images should not be reduced to the feelings of the patient. Feelings are not only personal but also belong to the imagined reality. That means that the images do not communicate other information, but rather depict in themselves a valid reality, which we can only refer to. If we follow this understanding, feelings are essentially personified images or archetypes, of which Hillman says: 'These inner persons keep our character in order, by giving a significant frame to every segment of our behaviour and our patterns of behaviour, which we call emotions, memories, motives, and attitudes' (1975, p. 128).

More recent developments of the archetype concept are referred to in the following chapter because they mostly refer to and attempt to integrate more recent research results.

4 Research on the archetype concept and resulting further developments of the theory

As was explained above, a central problem with Jung's archetype concept is that many different entities are denoted as archetypal: inner figures, mental processes, problematic situations between people, collective behaviour patterns, and 'instinctive' reactions. The whole debate about the archetype concept in analytical psychology is characterised by a lack of theoretical clarification and systematisation of what is precisely meant by the term archetype. What is also problematic from a scientific perspective is that Jung's claim that the archetype is in itself abstract, impossible to visualise, and never consciously perceivable has made this concept immune to every empirical review. Such a theory can no longer be falsified. It is true that Jung speaks continually of the archetype's existence as an empirical fact, but the use of the term 'empirical' surely no longer conforms to the present-day understanding of it in scientific psychology. This fact has certainly also contributed to the empirical investigation of the archetype concept being at least impeded. Below, an attempt will be made to extract a set of central tenets about the archetype from the different conceptualisations in order to then confront them with empirical research. Shelburne (1988) has dedicated some effort towards investigating the question of whether Jung's theory can in fact be labelled overall as a scientific theory and comes to the conclusion, at least concerning the theory of the archetype, that we cannot unconditionally confirm that it is.

DOI: 10.4324/9781003058458-4

This is all the more surprising since the beginnings of analytical psychology and Jung's occupation with psychology in general lay in empirical research. In his association studies, Jung discovered his concept of the complexes and the distinction between extroversion and introversion, and in principle had already experimentally proved at that time the existence of a dynamic unconscious. Ultimately it was also an essential point of why Freud was so interested in Jung. Freud was full of enthusiasm when he wrote about Jung in a letter: 'With that begins a new branch of empirical psychology' (Freud & Jung 1974, p. 538). The break with Freud and his retirement from university psychiatry, which also signified a fundamental break in Jung's own biography, were connected with his total rejection of this type of research. Thereafter, empirical research in Jungian psychology lay idle for decades and also long after Jung's death (with very few exceptions, see also Bash 1988).

An ambivalence has to be pointed out here, which runs throughout Jung's work and that persists even today in analytical psychology. This tension becomes apparent, on the one hand, when we consider the break in Jung's scientific biography. Jung was, as of 1906 at the latest, one of the most internationally well-known and most successful psychologists conducting empirical research thanks to his association studies. He gave this up, without ever again concerning himself with research in similar ways. Jung was surely an unusual personality, but even when this is factored in, it is an astounding change in his life to completely give up, almost overnight, research activity which had not only helped Jung gain international recognition, but which he had also pursued with a high degree of engagement and epistemological interest, and as a consequence to choose a completely interpretative approach to psychology. It is also in no way the case that Jung's research with the association experiment would have reached a limit in terms of content. It was quite the opposite; Jung may have been able to prove the existence of his central concept of the archetype by continuing down a fully empirical path.

The tension mentioned above also becomes apparent in Jung's work between the claim that his concepts are scientifically and empirically sound on the one hand and his exclusively her-meneutic approach on the other. Jung claims repeatedly, for example, that his concepts, such as the Anima, are empirical facts. This use of the term 'empirical', however, surely corres-ponds neither to the current understanding in scientific psych-ology nor to that of Jung's own time (Karl Popper had, for example, already begun to explore the logic of science and empiricism of the Vienna Circle in his publications in the 1920s and had formulated his concept of falsificationism as well as his so-called 3 Worlds theory, which is particularly interesting for analytical psychology, at the latest by the start of the thirties; Jung had not explicitly concerned himself which such things, but he could have known about them.). Elsewhere Jung insists that the archetypes must be understood as a biological fact. As is demonstrated above, Jung could not resolve the resulting contradictions throughout the course of his life. At this point I want to make it clear that Jung, at least in part, demonstrates in his work a very idiosyncratic understanding of science and empiricism, and has given little effort to connect his theories to contemporary knowledge and methodological approaches. Jung offers an interesting commentary to this problem of the excessive internal orientation, which is, however, presumably not related to himself, that namely the introvert

> is surely aligned to the inner and eternal meaning of the event, it is, however, maladjusted to actual reality. With this it removes its effectiveness, because it remains incompre-hensible. Its language is not that which is generally spoken, but rather a language that is too subjective, its arguments lack the convincing reason.
>
> (Jung CW 6, p. 731)

Even when Jung was in an intensive exchange with other scientists, he could not allow his concepts to be corrected by expert criticism, for example, in the discussion with the biolo-gist Portmann mentioned above. At the same time, he changes his archetype concept some years later without reference to Portmann, in that he introduced the concept of the not archetype in itself, but archetype as such, with which he tried to deal with the problems Portmann had identified (Shamdasani 2003).

On the other hand, Jung obviously kept up to date with the scientific knowledge in his field throughout his life by regularly reading the *Archives of General Psychiatry* (Personal disclosure from Tony Frey-Wehrlin). He was, therefore, well informed about the current body of knowledge which is, however, not at all reflected in his own publications. In any case it can be maintained that Jung moved throughout his life between the two poles of 'normal science' and interpretative, depth psychology, or even transcendentalism. In the terminology of modern social science this tension is described with the distinction between nomothetic (oriented around general regularities) and idiographic (oriented around the individual perspective of the subject and the individuality of the single case) research, and is reflected in the research logic of empirical falsificationism on the one hand and hermeneutics on the other. If Jung must be reproached in many areas for the fact that he switches back and forth between these discourses without reflection and creates contradictions, it must also be considered that he was able to transcend this tension in part in a very fruitful way – we only have to think of his concepts of synchronicity or Unus Mundus. This whole problem of his work can be found in its most prominent form in the analysis of the archetype concept.

In the meantime, however, numerous authors from analytical psychology have dealt with the concept of archetypes based on the latest scientific theories and research findings, which for some authors has also led to considerable modifications of the theory of archetypes. This debate will be presented in the following sections. To this end, however, in light of the above, an attempt should be made to systematically formulate scientifically verifiable elements of Jung's archetype concept.

4.1 Scientifically verifiable elements of Jung's term 'archetype'

If considered scientifically, Jung's theory about archetypes presents a hypothesis which should ideally be verifiable within the nomothetic, falsificationism paradigm and should, therefore, be falsifiable. I want to comment here, that for me this theoretical approach to knowledge is not the only valid one. In contrast, I myself have conducted systematic interpretative investigations of the archetype concept and take this to be essentially the most productive approach (see Roesler 2005, 2006). If the question of whether a theoretically claimed construct exists in empirical reality is to be investigated, however, it needs a nomothetic approach. I want now, therefore, to attempt to break Jung's concept down into component parts in order to present the results of empirical research on these individual points. One criticism of the approaches previously taken to reviewing the archetype concept as a scientific theory within analytical psychology is that too often the existence of a kind of archetype is considered as a given fact by Jungian authors, and appropriate theories and knowledge for this are then searched for (see e.g., Knox 2001, p. 628). Instead, the starting point should contain the possibility that the whole concept can also be false and nothing of the kind exists. Additionally, the numerous individual cases in analytical psychology are indeed a justifiable form of empirical investigation, but cannot be used to check the theoretical assertion of general laws (the problem of induction).

Jung's statements on the concept of the archetype can generally be summarised, in my opinion, in the following statements:

1 In the human psyche there is an a priori, therefore not gained through personal experience (or culturally passed down), basic pattern of experience and behaviour which is common for all people (universal) and that, if triggered in certain circumstances, structures the individual psychic phenomenon according to a general type, something collectively consistent.

2 The archetype presents a (largely) content empty basic structure which in different situations or in different cultures or time periods is filled with different concretisations. A consistent basic pattern remains, however, clearly recognisable.

3 This basic pattern is inherent and therefore a part of human genetic make-up.

4 The predisposition and the mode of operation of archetypes function analogously to instincts, in particular to the innate release mechanism in animals.

4.2 Empirical evidence for archetypes

4.2.1 *Association studies: corresponding interindividual core complexes*

Jung delivered one of the first pieces of empirical evidence for the idea that there must be archetypal patterns at the beginning of his scientific work in his association studies (Jung, CW 2). This was likewise one of the ways in which he more broadly came across the idea of archetypes. Here, Jung examined the reaction of test subjects to certain emotionally significant terms under experimental conditions. Jung was able to show in strictly empirical terms that there are unconscious, affectively loaded, and partially autonomous impacting factors in the human psyche, which he called complexes. By comparing many subjects, it became apparent that there are a series of complexes which correspond interindividually in their core contents. This corresponding core was then later described by Jung as the pre-image or archetype. From the standpoint of scientific research of Jungian concepts, it is extremely disappointing that Jung did not continue with these association studies after 1912 since he was in the process of providing evidence of supra-individual design factors of the individual and unconscious formation of complexes in a strictly empirical way. Here Jung reached the empirical conclusion that a) there are unconscious thematic complexes that revolve around a thematic core and that b) by examining a greater number of individuals, their complexes fall into a limited number of categories and there is, therefore, from a large number of studied individuals, only a limited number of continually repeating thematic cores. Jung's hypothesis here is: in the core of these categories an archetype is found which directs individuals' experience and which produces supra-individual similarity. Saunders and Skarr (2001) have recently taken up and continued this line of argument for a mathematical definition of the archetype: archetypes are the complexes, which fall statistically into the same categories.

4.2.2 *Proof for inherent mental structures*

Cross-cultural research shows that there is an inherent, universal set of clearly distinct basic emotions, which are already present in infants and which are also clearly recognisable from person to person, regardless of cultural differences (e.g., through facial expression) (Ekman et al. 1987).

Linguistic research shows that children have innate abilities to learn languages more easily. In the 1960s neurologists could show, through their efforts to model artificial language learning systems, that children could never, from the examples of language which they hear in their early years, reach the level of linguistic competence that they actually achieve if these rules were gained alone on a trial-and-error basis. Noam Chomsky (1978) deduced that a disposition to recognise and learn linguistic rules (e.g., syntax) more quickly than randomly must exist in the neural structure, which has since been described as the 'language acquisition device'. That such a system exists has since then been empirically proved. For example, a toddler, when presented with an as yet unknown object and is next given also an as yet unknown word, will interpret and use this word as a description for the object, while for an already known object, the new term will be understood as a description for a part of the object.

Newborns are obviously endowed with certain rudimentary perception and behaviour programmes, which are genetically fixed. In some cases, the gene responsible can even be identified. The cognitive biologists Johnson and Morton (1991, quoted in Knox 2003) describe a genetically fixed behavioural pattern whose genetic code is known and that they call CONSPEC. It makes newborn humans fixate on structures which match the human face longer than other objects. Infants are also able to differentiate relatively quickly in their first few weeks if a moving object was moved by an outside force or has moved itself and therefore must be a living being. All of these innate talents share the fact that they orient newborns above all around the interaction with other humans or initiate, support, or make an interaction easier (first and foremost with a caregiver). At this point it can at least be recorded that Jung has scored at least one victory over the paradigm of behaviourism, which was dominant in his time and is only now slowly losing its influence: the psyche of newborn infants is not a 'tabula rasa' and there are innate mental structures. This is also recognised increasingly in scientific psychology. Klaus Grawe, whom I would like to describe here as a 'reformed behaviouralist', has developed a so-called neuro-psychotherapy which is based, for example, on a model of innate, universal basic needs, which also includes attachment needs. Attachment research delivers more generally clear evidence for innate behaviour patterns amongst humans. All human infants form a close emotional relationship to at least one other person in the course of the first few months of their lives, which is essential for their psychological development and indeed for their survival. The characteristics of this relationship, as well as the conditions in which they are formed and their further development, are universally demonstrable. It was possible to prove in cross-cultural research of psychological development that all over the world there are four similar patterns of how children form attachments to their attachment figure (Cassidy & Shaver 2018).

Stevens (2003), therefore, connects his biological archetype concept with attachment theory and argues that archetypes are innate needs such as, for example, the need for attachment. Archetypes lie grounded in the homogeneity of basic human experiences, for example, the helplessness and dependence of the infant on the mother, which lead to particular and similar reactions in the brain. Evidence for this would be the universal validity of types of attachment.

4.2.3 *Anthropological research*

Ethnographic studies were the first to provide systematic theorising and research of the archetype concept, historically even before Jung. In ethnology, the high level of convergence in the narrative motifs of ethnic groups living far apart from each other had long since been noted and set in motion, from around 1880 onwards, a decade-long debate on how this correspondence in fairy tales and myths could be explained (see Chapter 2.8). Here are just a few examples for illustration. In a comparative study of over 50 randomly selected cultures, the incest motive appeared in the mythology of 39 of them (Kluckkohn 1960). The majority of the folk tales known around the world can be arranged into a typology with the number of types remaining in double digits, and for each type instances can be found from completely different parts of the world (Aarne & Thompson 1964). The following coinciding mythological narratives belong to practically all peoples: the primordial chaos, the separation of the sky and the earth, a devouring flood as punishment for humanity, the incest of the original divine siblings, the theft of fire from the gods, and many others. As a result of the theoretical dispute between isolationism (fundamental thoughts) and diffusionism (migration hypothesis), intensive research in ethnography took place and knowledge about migratory movements and cultural exchange was indeed gained. Without a doubt, cultures have reciprocally influenced each other, and this has had an impact with regards to mythology and linguistics. In the second half of the twentieth century, the migration hypothesis in ethnography seemed to be disproved. It was not possible to prove physical contact between all ethnic groups with converging myths, and with some it was even explicitly ruled out. Since the rise of archaeogenetics, the situation has changed: with technical improvements in the sequencing of DNA from prehistoric human remains, mainly bones, it became possible to trace the migration routes of early Homo sapiens over the world. It became visible that there has been extensive exchange between groups of humans from the very beginning of homo sapiens around 200,000 years ago, and even across continents. So the similarities can now be well explained by migration and cultural exchange, whereas the differences between peoples are due to the separation of territories, mainly as a result of rising sea levels at the end of the Ice Age with the consequence of land bridges disappearing (e.g., the Bering Strait land bridge from Asia to America) (Witzel 2012).

Human ethnologists have identified a set of universal human behaviours in culturally comparative studies:

> Universals of social behaviour are observed in the following areas: in the mother-child relationship, in the search for a relationship, in the formation of a hierarchy, in territorial behaviour, in the ownership and exchange of objects, in intra-species as well as curiosity/explorative aggression.
>
> (Obrist 1990)

This is indeed one of the most convincing pieces of evidence for the existence of archetypes, but likewise these universals can also be explained without recourse to the claim that they are genetically inherited. Lévi-Strauss (1976) found a completely different explanation in his concept of structural anthropology: the intercultural homogeneity, for example, in marriage and initiation rituals, arises because human societies at all times and all over the world are confronted with the same structural problems (e.g., the detachment from strong emotional ties to the original family and the opening to new bonds, which allow for healthy procreation, therefore not constituting incest and so securing the continuation of the society) and then find similar solutions for these problems.

Furthermore, contrary arguments with a wide array of evidence can be found in the work of other anthropologists. Ahnert (2010), for example, shows that such massive intercultural differences exist in even the most basic human characteristics and behaviours, for example, in caregiving behaviour, that it is not possible to speak of universals here. In my opinion, there is also the problem that Jungians like to select those research results which support Jung's theory of archetypes and often reject material which does not fit.

4.2.4 *Research on altered states of consciousness*

Studies which relate to altered states of consciousness were already being cited as early as the 1960s and 1970s as evidence for the validity of archetype theory: Masters and Houston

(1966) documented the fantasies of test subjects under the effects of LSD and mescaline in 206 sessions conducted under experimental conditions over a period of 15 years. On the one hand, they reported a high level of regularity in the patterns of the reported fantasies. The examiners were frequently perceived as distorted in very similar ways, namely as gods, priests, or people of wisdom, truth, or beauty, and therefore seen as numinous, which matches the definition of archetypes. On the other hand, the reported fantasies correspond to a high degree with mythological themes (the myth of the child-hero, of creation, of eternal return, of paradise and the Fall, of incest and punishment); polarities (light and dark, order and chaos, myths of the grail quest); and the occurring figures were religious figures in 96% of the cases. Similar results were reported by Stanislaf Grof (1978) from his experiments with LSD. It is argued that the hallucinogen moves the nervous system of the test subjects into an interindividually similar state and activates the phylogenetic, congenial neural structures, in other words, the archetypes. The fantasies which are experienced are forms of the archetypal basic pattern. From a scientific perspective, this line of argument is problematic in that it contains a high level of interpretation and it could be accused of reading into the material what it wants to find. Also, all test subjects were of course adults and had, therefore, gone through a process of socialisation. It could be said that the homogeneity or similarity of the images is grounded in the similarity of their cultural influences. Consequently, the thesis of inherent archetypal images cannot be proved. On the other hand, the similarity of the reported fantasies is indeed notable. The American Jungian John Ryan Haule (2010) has recently commented extensively on Jung's archetype concept in a comprehensive two-volume work and has collected a wealth of theoretical and empirical data. An example would be the so-called causal operator, therefore the human trait of creating causal connections, in which Haule recognises even the foundations of modern science. Haule's theses on the neuropsychological foundation of certain rituals and ritual body postures, how they can be found all over the world and that they depict a universal form of human behaviour, is very interesting. Haule supports himself with the research of the anthropologist Felicitas Goodman (1992), who conducted comparative ritual research. From these comparisons she extrapolated certain widespread universal body postures, as they are used by different tribes to achieve a state of trance. These body postures were then assumed by participants in experimental studies, and it appears that the poses lead to trance states which can be relatively reliably differentiated from one another. What is particularly interesting is that these poses can be found as depictions in Neolithic cave paintings. Goodman and Haule assume that human beings had earlier discovered these poses as effective in inducing trances because the poses use determined universal conditions of the human neural system. That these poses are on the one hand widespread and on the other hand also trigger trance states in humans today suggests that here they must actually have something to do with universal patterns. The rooting of these patterns in the body can also be proved. In a study, Rittner (2006) was able to depict the state of consciousness triggered through the trance poses in an electroencephalogram. Here, a characteristic phenomenon appears, namely an increase in cortical negation (which indicates an observably high tension) with a simultaneous increase of slow theta waves, which are associated with deep relaxation. What is seen, therefore, is a paradoxical state of the brain which is far outside that of everyday experience. What is interesting from a Jungian perspective is that here Jung's differentiation between the ultimately inexperienceable, content-empty 'archetype in-itself' as well as the concrete archetypal image that it is not possible to experience can again be found. The ritual body poses are the same amongst all tribes and trigger corresponding trances, and the contents of the 'spirit travels' are then, however, each culturally dependent – the Inuit meets the seal spirit, the pygmy meets the spirit animals of the African jungle.

Haule (2010) argues, in light of this, that archetypes must be understood as 'typical emotional bodily conditions' (p. 259). These conditions are an evolutionary contingent-specific combination of conditions of the neural system, in particular the autonomous nervous system, coming from the release of hormones and neuromodulators, postures, facial expressions, and so on. Human groups would have previously learned to differentiate these conditions and above all to develop rituals and myths with which these conditions could be brought about with certainty.

That there are obviously influences of archetypal patterns on body states is also proved in the following study. In a study of pain medicine, Kut et al. (2007) asked test subjects to identify with certain archetypal role models (originally described as such) and to measure the magnitude of the pain they experienced. It became apparent that for those who identified with the image of a hero or heroine, the subjective experience of pain was significantly less apparent than for those test subjects who had identified with a coward. The authors intend to use this knowledge in the treatment of chronic pain syndromes.

4.2.5 Experimental studies on archetypal memory

In order to obtain a means of being able to objectively and systematically investigate the archetype hypothesis, David Rosen and his team at the department for analytical psychology at Texas A&M University developed the Archetypal Symbol Inventory (ASI), which consists of 40 archetypal symbols and 40 connected words which indicate the archetypal meaning of these symbols (Rosen et al., 1991). Rosen and Smith also developed a series of experiments in order to test the hypothesis of an archetypal, meaning collectively unconscious, memory.

In the first study, whose design was borrowed from cognitive psychology research, Rosen et al. (1991) investigated associations between symbols and their meanings (Siefert (1975) had already indicated the productive link between the archetype concept and cognitive psychology research of learning systems). From laboratory research on learning and memory, it is known that associations between semantically connected terms (e.g., tree and leaf) are learned more easily than random couplings. In the study, the 'Archetypal Symbol Inventory' test was developed: 40 images of symbols, which in Jungian psychology are considered archetypes, were selected and each was combined with a word which denoted its archetypal meaning (e.g., the image 'Butterfly' and the meaning 'Soul'). The hypothesis was that these links, which consist of archetypal images and denotations, are able to be learnt more easily and therefore better remembered than random combinations because there is a predisposition in the brain for the archetypal combinations. In order to ensure that the 'archetypal' combinations were not strengthened through cultural influences, two pre-studies were conducted, which confirmed that there was no conscious knowledge of the links among the test subjects. It could, therefore, be assumed that all combinations were unknown and the chance to learn them was equally distributed. In the main study, 235 test subjects were presented with 40 combinations of images and words. In the second stage the test subjects were then asked to remember the related word when presented only with the image. Half of the combinations were in the right 'archetypal' combination, and the other half were 'wrongly' combined. The variance analysis evaluation clearly showed that the archetypal combinations were able to be learned more easily and with this the hypothesis was highly significantly confirmed ($p < .0001$). Further studies from Huston (1992) as well as Huston et al. (1999) with the original ASI found the same significant effects.

In order to assess whether the results of Rosen et al. show an effect which can be found in all cultural and linguistic contexts, Sotirova-Kohli et al. (2013) translated the ASI into German and carried out a replication of the study in German-speaking Switzerland. The results showed the same significant effects as those in the American studies, thereby proving the cross-cultural validity of the hypothesis of an archetypal memory.

The same lead author had already previously (Sotirova-Kohli et al. 2011) transferred the rationale of the ASI to another medium, namely Japanese characters, and examined them with the same research design as the original American study. What is specific about kanji, that makes it particularly suited for the investigation of archetypal memory, is that they were originally Chinese characters based on pictorial representations which were then taken over into Japanese. It emerged as a semiotic system that is independent of language. The investigation is based on the assumption that, given the circumstances of its origin as well as the peculiarity of their cognitive processing as part of the system of the Japanese language, kanji represent symbolic archetypal images (image schemata). Chinese images in the Japanese language do not function phonetically, but rather have retained their denotive worth as images that trigger an unconscious/implicit knowledge of meanings in the language system, similar to the archetypal symbols of the ASI. The nature of the Japanese language makes possible in this sense a relation to the archetypal level, independent of the phonetic signifiers of the language, by means of a graphical representation of the language concepts using Chinese characters.

The authors utilised a series of 40 kanji and conducted the same series of three experiments as Rosen at al. (1991). Initially, two pilot studies were conducted (Experiments 1 and 2), in order to check if the participants, who had not learned any Asian languages with Chinese characters, were able to recognise the meaning of the symbols by drawing on cryptomnestic knowledge. Both prior studies showed little to no prior knowledge of the meaning of the characters. In the main part of the study Sotirova-Kohli et al. (2011) assumed that if kanji characters, like archetypal images (Rosen et al., 1991), are connected with their correct meaning, these correct pairs would have a better learning and retrieval rate than for a connection with an incorrect meaning. Here too, it was possible to significantly prove the effect of the 'correct' combination of symbol and meaning, and a better learning or reproduction rate was apparent, which, in the same sense as above, can be taken as evidence for an archetypal memory.

In an attempt to explain the results on a neuroscientific and cognitive psychological level, Huston et al. (1999) argue that there is possibly a mechanism for the evolutionary, collective (archetypal) memory. They explain the effect of the better retrieval of meanings if they are paired with the correct symbols as the result of an inter-hemispherical connection which is mediated by the corpus callosum. This enables the exact meaning of the archetypal symbol, which is triggered by an affective reaction, to be retrieved (Huston et al. 1999, pp. 145–146). According to Huston, the right side of the brain is the residence of archetypal patterns and symbols as well as their affectively charged images, while the left side of the brain contains verbal knowledge. When someone is shown an archetypal symbol in connection with the correct meaning, an affective reaction will be triggered, which is connected with a certain archetypal image in the right hemisphere and that leads the evolutionary, unconscious, and archetypal memory to be stimulated. It is, therefore, the affective reaction which makes the retrieval of the correct meaning (word) of the symbol easier if the symbols are later shown alone.

The assumption investigated here and the construction of the study are very similar to Seligman's (1972) concept of 'preparedness' and his related studies, which showed that in mammals as well as in humans, a biologically innate disposition to learn exists. Humans, for example, develop phobias based only on certain stimuli, like spiders or snakes, and not like doves or hares. Seligman interprets this as also being dependent on evolution and not biologically inherent.

In another, also experimental, study by Maloney (1999), the same explanatory hypothesis, namely that images with archetypal content trigger in adults a specific structure of preferences for that image, was tested in other ways. As a basis, the following assumptions derived from archetype theory were used:

> First, innate structure must affect subjects' emotional responses. Second, archetypal effects must be sufficiently discrete to be detected as separate processes. Third, archetypal structure must affect adult perception. Fourth, visual images presented must be related to archetypal themes. And finally, questions presented to subjects must be evocative of the underlying archetypal structure.
>
> (p. 103)

The 151 subjects were presented with images of the two archetypal themes 'Mother' and 'Hero', with three versions in each: positive, negative, and non-anthropomorphic (in a non-human form). The subjects had to perform a Q-sort, thus arranging the images in order of preference for certain questions, for example, the question 'I perceive this picture as ... (very unpleasant to very pleasant)'. The combinations matching every question were checked using Bartlett's sphericity test to see whether they significantly differ from a random order, where the significance test was very strictly set with p < .005. In this test only one question (Q3) showed itself to be significant, but it was nevertheless consistent and significant to a high degree in all three versions: 'If I had to always carry this image with me, it would be ... (very unpleasant to very pleasant) for me'. The authors interpreted this to mean that evidently only this question brought forth a reaction to the image that was accordingly strong enough so that an archetypal structure comes into effect. The combinations of Q3 then underwent a factor analysis, which gave the same three factor structures in each of the three versions. The author interpreted this as consistent with archetype theory and evidence for its validity.

4.2.6 Research with the archetype concept

Aside from the question of its empirical justification, the archetype concept has been used in numerous empirical research projects.

On the basis of the archetype concept, standardised test instruments have been developed. Here, the Pearson-Marr Archetype Indicator (PMAI) (Pearson & Marr 2003, 2007) in particular should be highlighted, for which satisfactory test-quality criteria and evaluation manuals for various areas of application are available and that now has a wide application, predominantly in the areas of organisation and management. The test is generally accessible as an online version from the website of the Centre for Applications of Psychological Type (www.capt.org), which also hosts trainings and runs a databank about research using PMAI. Numerous empirical studies on the relationship between Jung's typology and the concept of archetypes can be found in the literature database on this website and in the journals *Bulletin of Psychological Type, Journal of Psychological Type, Australian Journal of Psychological Type,* and *British Association for Psychological Type, TypeFace.*

Using the archetype concept and respective operationalisations, the influence of archetypal factors on different contexts was empirically investigated, including on weight loss (Twillman 2000) and athletic performance (Dench 2007), among others. Boyd's comprehensive research programme (1991) must most notably be highlighted for its research on the contribution of small groups to individual development on the basis of Jungian psychology. Within this framework, an operationalisation was developed based on the comprehensive Jungian literature on the concept of the archetypes Animus and Anima, with which the occurrence of these archetypes in group interactions was able to be empirically understood. From the perspective of clinical psychology, Alexopoulou (2008) researched a subsample of families from a Europe-wide comparative study of systemic family therapy and psychodynamic short-term therapy for families with children diagnosed with depression. In this study, the 'Archetypal family therapy' approach developed by Papadopoulos (1996) was used in order to analyse the clinical proceedings from an archetypal perspective.

Many authors have concerned themselves with the influence of archetypal factors overcoming transition stages in life or critical life events and with this have also examined Jung's concept of the individuation process as an archetypal structure of development over the life course. Pedersen-Shaefer (2002) allocated the female archetypes, according to Bolen (1984), to 153 middle-aged, female subjects and investigated, using standardised, clinical test instruments, (SCL-90-R, Quality of Life Questionnaire) their stress levels and mental strain. An interesting result here is that the women who were assigned a female archetype which is unvalued in our culture (e.g., Persephone or Demeter), experienced more global stress, while the women with a more highly valued archetype, experienced more anxiety. Prendergast (2005), however, researched middle-aged men based on in-depth interviews and was able to determine that this transition was experienced as more difficult than all previous transitions for all subjects. The transition could clearly be better overcome if feelings could be communicated and the person had a spiritual orientation. Oxidine (2001) researched the conscious and unconscious experience of the individuation process in over-65-year-olds on the basis of the 'grounded-theory' methodology.

All of these authors interpreted their results as proof of Jung's perception of an archetypal structure in the individuation process.

4.2.7 Discussion of the empirical evidence

It can be determined, based on our present-day level of knowledge, that there are evidently verifiably universal, innate, or at least (neuro-)psychologically grounded abilities or qualities in humans on a mental level. The overview also shows that the archetype concept can certainly be operationalised in scientific research in a verifiable manner. The overview of the level of research makes it clear on the other hand, however, that the number of these universal, mental traits is very limited and these are also restricted to very simple, basic mental competencies. This is a first, central point where contemporary scientific knowledge at least calls into question Jung's original conception of archetypes: the verifiable 'archetypal' qualities are in their level of complexity far too simple and very far away from something so complex as, for example, the myth of the hero's journey. This issue has also been noted by current Jungian authors but discussed in diverse ways. The American Jungian John Ryan Haule (2010) has recently commented on Jung's archetype concept in a comprehensive two-volume work and pulled together a wealth of theoretical and empirical data. He persistently highlights Jung's prescient insights and their convergence with modern knowledge but has also collected material which contradicts Jung on several points. His general argument is that there is now enough evidence in the natural sciences for the existence of an archetypal structure. As a prominent example for a biologically grounded archetype, he uses the human ability for language. For this there actually appears to be a biologically grounded disposition (see above: 'language acquisition device'). Haule overlooks in my opinion, however, that the archetypes he highlights, such as language, for which there is scientific evidence, are very small in number and are also far from many of the concepts that Jung himself described as archetypal. As mentioned above, this also includes complex social behaviour patterns and mythical narratives, amongst others. Haule attempts to counter these problems with the term 'symbolic penetration' of biogenetic structuralism. He argues that myths and rituals are conceived in such a way that they address certain universal neural structures in humans and therefore bring forth similar intercultural reactions. This argument has also already been considered from a scientific perspective, as shown below.

Bischof (1996) examined in detail the analogy archetype-inborn release mechanism (AAM) using the 'child schema' from ethology (Eibl-Eibesfeldt 1987) and the archetype of the (divine) child (Jung CW 9/1), to test whether parallels can be drawn between ethology and psychology. The so-called 'child schema' consists of the idea that for most animal species the head of the young animal is bigger in relation to the body and the face is compacter, therefore meaning a squat nose or that the eyes, nose, and mouth are closer together and so on. This form presents a trigger for the adult individual that inhibits aggression and activates caregiving behaviour, amongst other reactions. Bischof contrasts Jung's explanations on the child archetype, in particular the pictorial representations in which the child appears. His conclusion:

> These two patterns of interpretation are poles apart [...]
> For the ethological concept the central point of interest is evidently the physiognomic appearance of the child form. There are very definite formal characteristics which must fit like a key in a lock of the perceptual filter which should trigger the nurturing behaviour.
>
> (Bischof 1996, p. 121f)

For the pictorial representations, which Jung researched as manifestations of the child archetype, the child carried a symbolic meaning which is transmitted through the spatial symbolism:

> The child is a carrier of meaning who is not at all interested in how he looks, but rather only that he is in the middle of the image and that he is enclosed on all sides by a protective, uterine shell. It is easy to imagine that a diamond in a chest, a pearl in a mussel, a precious elixir in a retort evoke similar images and therefore these pictures are also named by Jung as possible alternatives.
>
> (p. 122)

The problem is, therefore, that Jung places two entities in parallel which lie on categorically different levels. On the one hand is an instinctive pattern of behaviour, almost on the level of a reflex, and on the other hand is a more or less complex symbolic structure of meaning. Precisely this issue runs throughout Jung's whole argument on archetypes. Bird behaviour patterns cannot be equated with complex, meaningful patterns such as rituals or mythological stories in humans.

It should be added that the behavioural biologists of Jung's time assumed that the complete behavioural pattern is genetically determined. This seems possible for more primitive species of animals, but for mammals it becomes questionable – see for example, Harlow's studies of apes, which show that a lack of mothering in childhood leads to adult apes being unable to show any caregiving behaviour to their own offspring. Similarly, the large intercultural variability in caregiving and child nurturing behaviour among humans is relevant here. What is problematic, is that biologists in that time had, from today's perspective, a very fragmented picture of genetics, which Jung took on completely. As to the question of whether or not archetypes can be genetically fixed, therefore, the current insights into human genetics in Chapter 4.3.1 should be referred to.

In the overview of the current level of knowledge it will also be clear that previous authors writing on analytical psychology have handled the documentary evidence for archetype theory very selectively and have not regarded opposing evidence or even have actively eliminated it. It is possible that until today, the role of biology in the transmission of certain mental traits has been overestimated in analytical psychology and that cultural influences have been systematically underestimated. More than once, the differences in psychological characteristics between the genders are evidently traced back chiefly to biological differences, rather than as being mainly a product of learning and socialisation, and depending, therefore, principally on cultural and social influences. The psychologist Cordelia Fine (2010) has made these influencing factors evident in a series of sophisticated experiments. Women perform just as well as men in mathematics tests, for example, when it is explained to them beforehand that there would be no difference between men and women in such tests. If the women are told before, however, that 'men are just simply better at mathematics tests', then the women also perform significantly worse. The influence of expectations, here gender stereotypes, becomes even more drastic if the women complete the tests dressed in bathing suits. Then they perform clearly worse than if they had been dressed in normal clothing. The gender differences, therefore, which can be empirically found, are actually more dependent on culturally determined expectations than biological factors. Another field in which universal convergences have always been suspected is in childcare. Lieselotte Ahnert (2010), the leading German researcher in the area of infant psychology, has proven in a culturally comparative study that there is no universal type of an original form of childcare. Instead, more differences than similarities can be found between cultures. This also seems to be the case amongst traditional peoples, which Jung always assumed would be closer to the archetypes. The only universal similarities are in the field of attachment; here biologically innate processes seem to actually be present.

There also remains, finally, the argument that other explanations for the alignment in human behaviour or in mythology can be found, explanations which are regularly not taken into account by Jungian authors. There is, to my knowledge, for example, no detailed discussion from the Jungian side on Claude Lévi-Strauss' (1976) structural anthropology, although this deals with precisely the same questions as Jung, albeit from a social science perspective.

On the other hand, there are multiple empirical indications, even in the experimental studies mentioned here, that there must be something like archetypes, independent of the question how they come into being. In essence, the controversy surrounding the understanding of Jung's archetypes is always based on the question of how the archetypes are transferred from generation to generation. At this point in the discussion it should have become clear, that the critical question of the archetype concept revolves around how the universality of the archetypal pattern is achieved. Jung – and until now a large circle of authors in analytical psychology – argues that they are innate and would be passed on via genetic pathways. The insights and research mentioned above, however, makes it clear that evidently some competencies defined as archetypal only link together in the processes of development from various basic components. The question of how these processes can be explained in a more detailed way defines the present debate surrounding the archetype concept. This will now be discussed against the background of contemporary insights in human genetics and the genetic transmission of mental qualities.

4.3 Explanatory approaches for the emergence and the transference of archetypes

4.3.1 *State of the art in human genetics and epigenetics*

Jung argues that archetypes can be located in the genetic make-up of human beings. We have already seen that exactly what is meant by archetypes must be precisely discerned. It makes an enormous difference if it is claimed that the pattern of how the weaver bird builds its nest, for example, is genetically innate, or if a complex mythological concept, some cognitive content, is genetically coded. The second is simply not possible. Since the complete mapping of the human genome as part of the Human Genome Project, we know that the human genetic make-up is limited to around 24,000 genes and these are engaged for the large part with the construction of organs (Bauer 2008). Moreover, genes encode only the construction of certain proteins, which in turn entails certain biological processes. If 'Nature' really attempted to code such complex symbolic information like, for example, a mythological image, an unbelievable amount of 'storage space' would be needed for it – without even looking at the question of whether this is indeed even possible. The existing genes would never be sufficient to achieve the coding of that which is conceptualised as archetypes in Jung's theory. Human geneticists are very clear in their assertion that genes cannot serve as carriers of complex symbolic information. Only subcortical structures arise through genetic control in early human development. Symbolic information, however, needs networks in the neocortex that only form in the course of development, well beyond the first year of life (Knox 2003). That means that archetypes in the sense of complex symbolic structures, so for example, mythologems like the myth of the hero, fundamentally cannot be genetically coded and the actually existing innate mental structures are so rudimental, or only oriented around sensory perception, that they are miles away from these complex symbolic patterns.

There have already been all kinds of attempts by Jung and others after him to rescue the biologic and genetic concept of archetypes. Jung was also to some extent conscious of the problem that symbolic information cannot be genetically coded. He made a distinction, therefore, from 1947 between the archetype-as-such, which is only a core and empty of content, and the concrete archetypal image, where there is indeed culturally different content. Unfortunately, Jung was extremely vague here regarding what the archetype-as-such is and where it can be located (e.g., 'transmitted by Mendelian particles'). We must also ask the question here of whether structures of the archetype-as-such can even be conceived of as empty of content, or if each mental structure is always defined by its content.

Jung's assertion of a genetically invested complex archetype is based on the fragmented knowledge of genetics in his time. The actual way in which genes function, as we know today, is clearly distinct from the notion which Jung assumes as a basis and which also appears in many current arguments. This outdated idea can perhaps be formulated as simply as follows: the genetic code is synonymous with a blueprint, in that the whole construction of a human being and also their brain is predetermined and this blueprint is only read and implemented in early development.

It has actually been found in recent years that there are different mechanisms by which genes interact with their environment, and that biological and genetic structures can be even changed through social and mental influences during development (Bauer 2008, 2006, 2005, 2002). Most notably described are two mechanisms, DNA-methylation and histone modification, which are labelled in summary as epigenetics (Buiting 2005). Put simply, genes are not only comprised of information for the construction of certain proteins (coding unit), but include a sequence which can receive signals from the environment in a biochemical way (initially from the direct environment of the cell, but also from the person's environment through neuro-biochemical signal transmission) and implement this in a gene's activation or deactivation – a gene switch or promoter. A gene is, then, not simply carried out like a blueprint, but rather it is switched on and off depending on the environmental conditions, something that is described as 'gene expression'. This 'gene switch' can be 'packaged' either through the coiling of the histone or by adding methyl groups. Both processes have the effect that the 'gene switch' is less easily accessible or even completely unreachable and that therefore the gene can be less easily or not at all read. The most interesting thing about this new insight is that this 'packaging' can be altered through early experiences within the uterus and in the first months of life. An example would be the modification of the reaction to stress (Bauer 2006, Meaney 2010): maternal care in the first months of life leads to various neuro-biochemical intermediate steps to remove the methyl groups from the gene switch of the glucocorticoid receptor gene, which means that the gene is permanently accessible for reading. This causes a permanently lower level of stress hormones (e.g., cortisol) and thus represents a permanent buffer against stress.

Francis Collins, one of the leaders of the Human Genome Project and one of the world-leading human geneticists, summarises the current insight in the interaction of predispositions and the environment when he writes 'that the gene builds the basis on which the environment has an impact' (Collins 2011, p. 231) and cites his colleague Matt Ridley:

> Genes are neither puppeteers nor blueprints. And they are not simply hereditary factors. They are active throughout life, they switch both on and off, they react to the environment. They may control the structure of the body and brain in the womb, but then they disassemble and rebuild everything that they have already established – solely in reaction to external stimuli. They are at the same time the origins as well as the results of our activities. Sometimes the supporters of the 'environmental side' are so frightened by the strength and inevitability of the genes that they overlook the most important message: the genes are on their side.
>
> (Collins 2011, p. 231)

This last observation plays on the famous debate of 'Nurture or Nature' which has essentially dominated the discussion in numerous sciences, for example, in developmental psychology, throughout the twentieth century. With regard to this debate, it could now actually be argued that this question, namely of whether or not a biological system or environmental factors are prevalent in the formation of mental features, has basically been answered through the knowledge of epigenetics – both are correct, but the interesting question here is actually: how does the interaction between the two variables work?

Genetic research has now identified different gene variants which accompany mental features, but which nevertheless also integrate with environmental influences. Small variances in the 'depression gene' (5-HTTLPR), for example, increase the risk of depression – although only in conjunction with adverse childhood experiences. Belsky (2009) coined the term 'differential susceptibility' for this. For a detailed overview of the discussion, see Cassidy & Shaver 2018)

Taken together, these results mean one thing first and foremost: even when humans are without a doubt constructed with genetic information, experiences, especially those in the early stages of development and predominantly experiences in relationships with caregivers, essentially play a role in which genetic information can be read, and indeed how and when it is read (gene expression). 'Experience itself can modify the expression of genes' (Marcus 2004, p. 98). Haule (2010) moreover observes: 'Specifically, the genes whose expression is modified (turned on or off) are those that manufacture the proteins which alter the synapses, 'hardening' the wiring in some and 'softening' it in others' (p. 143). Experiences ultimately cause, therefore, a very different formation of the same genetic predispositions, and certain genes can be generally activated based on certain experiences. The key word of modern developmental theory (Developmental Systems Theory) is, therefore, no longer 'blueprint' but rather 'interaction'. The debate of 'Nurture or Nature' has therefore become obselete. Merchant (2012) has excellently summarised the implications of this insight for the theory of archetypes as well as how the current state of the debate between proponents of a fully biological grounding of archetypes versus supporters of an interactionalistic viewpoint. Interestingly, Merchant comes to the realisation in this recent work, through reviewing Jung's own case studies, with which he sought to prove the genetic predisposition of archetypes, that all of these classic case studies can also be explained without the stringent assumption of biologically inhereted archetypes (see Chapter 6). As a consequence, he takes on a position which can be described as 'emergence' and will be explained further below. A particularly important implication concerns the universality of archetypes. Jung thought that the archetypes would have to be present in the same way for all people and this is only guaranteed when the archetypes are genetically rooted. Present-day genetics calls this into question. Even if something is genetically predisposed, it in no way means that it also leads to the same characteristics in all gene carriers. As has been shown, this depends to a high degree on environmental influences, for example, if the gene can even be read, with the consequence that the statement: the same gene is present in multiple people, means hardly anything. This also means the argument, that archetypes arise from the same construction of the human brain, becomes obsolete because this similarity is in no way a given. If people have different experiences over the course of their lives, then they ultimately also have different brains because the experiences have an impact on the structure of the brain. In addition there is the insight into the high sensitivity of biological development to context conditions. Even the smallest influences can in the course of development trigger massive changes so that, even by optimal control of gene and environmental conditions, practically no predictions about the formation of features is possible. This clashes primarily with one of Jung's conceptions, which implicitly pervades his entire work. He contests that the individuality and the mental idiosyncrasy of a person are somehow innate, preformed, and independent from external influences – archetype theory is only the most prominent form of this underlying conception. This overemphasis on the autonomy of the individual and the interior is surely, to use Jung's own words, his 'personal equation'. Jung has made an enormous contribution to the rehabilitation of the interior and the imagination, of introversion and individual development in the psychology of our rather extroverted culture. This orientation had the downside, in my opinion, however, that it neglected for the most part the significance of relationships between people for development (with few exceptions, for example, *The Psychology of Transference*, Jung CW 16). Moreover, it can be said that the current insights of epigenetics only strengthen the significance of the environmental conditions, and in particular those of early relationships with caregivers, namely that the same genotype, dependent on the environmental conditions and here above all experiences in close relationships, leads to completely different formations, not only in the mental but also in terms of physical biology.

Other authors (e.g., Tresan 1996) have already accused Jung of an inappropriate reductionism in his attempts to find a biological foundation for archetypes. Stadler (1997) has worked out in detail how biographical influences were systematically disregarded in Jung's theorising. I assume that something else

lay behind Jung's decade-long effort to force his archetype concept into a biological conception. Jung (as well as Freud) was
very conscious that he would expose himself to considerable
criticism by developing a psychology of the unconscious in
an age of positivist-materialistic science (see also Shamdasani
2003). Likewise, both were evidently extremely influenced by
the advances of the 'hard' natural sciences in their time. This
is also evident, in my opinion, in Jung's attempt to align his
theory of psychic energy strictly to the laws of thermodynamics.
This applies, for example, to the laws of entropy, which is basic
for Jung's theory of the balance of psychic energy – ironically
these are considered now, at least in the form from Jung's time,
as being refuted, which astoundingly to my knowledge has not
been received in analytical psychology as it would have led to a
change in the very concept of energetics. In any case, this evidently led to Jung thinking that his theory would only be on
solid ground if he formulated it as a sort of natural science.
There is a curious tension to his practical scientific approach,
which is namely hermeneutic – and this tension runs through
his entire work. Jürgen Habermas (1968) charged Freudian
psychoanalysis with 'scientific self-misunderstanding', and the
same applies, in my opinion, to analytical psychology. Indeed,
all psychology is always concerned with meaning and as part
of this, the understanding of structures of meaning – which
Jung had clearly indicated with his emphasis on the centrality
of 'meaning' – and this employment cannot be thought of as
natural science, but rather it always needs the effort of an interpretative mind.

We are, therefore, facing a dilemma regarding the decisive
characteristics of the universal qualities of archetypes. The idea
of a genetic transmission path as a way of securing the universal
spread of archetypal information is no longer viable in light of
these new insights. How, then, can a path to the passing on of
universal, mental archetypes be theoretically conceptualised?

In what follows, current theories from different sciences will
be referred to, and these represent possible candidates for a
revised concept of explaining archetypes.

4.3.2 Endophenotypes

A possible solution for the dilemma potentially lies in the new theoretical concept of 'endophenotypes', which Staufenberg (2011) describes in the following terms:

> Endophenotypes (or also intermediate phenotypes) are a theoretical research concept and are a kind of bridge between the genotype, which can only be measured with molecular biology, and the visible and observable phenotype that it (also) produces. The phenotype is created not only through the genes and their complex transcriptions and gene-gene interactions, but rather also through epigenetic factors, therefore also through the influences of the environment.
>
> (p. 87)

The author attempts to use this concept to explain ADHD disorder. Here it is particularly clear that while there may be genetic predispositions that cause the formation of this condition, these are, however, not entirely sufficient for the disorder to manifest itself, but rather this requires something more, partially psychosocial factors. These in turn only result in an illness with the existence of the specific genetic predispositions. Here there is nevertheless evidently no infinite number of variable combinations, but rather typical combinations of genetic predispositions and environment conditions exist, which can be empirically found in these very combinations as the trigger of the disorder. For an account of archetypes this means that archetypes could be defined as such specific combinations of genetic predispositions with specific experiences. It is evident at present that in psychopathology there is not a limitless variety of conditions but rather typical 'syndromes' for which it is possible to find typical causal constellations, for example, the experience of separation/abandonment for depression. Evidently, a genetically contingent disposition must exist so that a person reacts to the experience with a specific disorder. That would explain why not all children who have matching experiences react with the formation of an analogous condition.

4.3.3   Concepts and research results from Gestalt psychology, cognitive science, and neuroscience

In the Berlin School of Gestalt Psychology (Metzger 1954) it was argued that it is a quality of our cognitive structure to form concise, coherent configurations and then to stabilise these, therefore resisting further changes. These 'good Gestalts' are therefore ubiquitous, which was also experimentally researched (Stadler & Kruse 1990). Subjects were presented with a dot pattern that they then had to reproduce from memory. This reproduction would then be presented to another participant, who must in turn reproduce it, and this in turn to another and so on. It was possible to observe that the additions at some point reached a stable configuration which did not change any further and that corresponded in the different series of subjects. The active principle behind this is described as 'convergence' and explains the corresponding forms that can be found everywhere in nature, which have such good adaptive properties in themselves that they can no longer be changed (e.g., the body forms of fish and whales, even though whales are mammals and have no relationship in evolutionary terms with fish). In the further development of the Gestalt theory, the convergence principle flows into the general theory of self-organising systems. This theory was in turn taken up in analytical psychology by Saunders and Skarr (2001) and applied to the archetype concept. They argue that where Jung says the archetype is only 'form without substance', he confuses it with the *process* which produces the similar patterns. The results of neuroscience, in particularly connectionist models, confirm that the information in the brain is not localised to one place, but rather to a greater degree in the coordinated activity of neural networks, and so in a process. According to Saunders and Skarr, the archetypes could be located in the processes of the brain's self-organisation which produce the mental pattern:

When we employ a dynamical systems view of development, we no longer need the archetype per se to explain the formation of complexes. In fact, we could do without it altogether and still have the same basic psychological system that Jung proposed.

(Skar 2004, p. 247)

This would mean, however, that archetypes are no longer fully pre-existing. The brain's forms of organisation establish themselves in conjunction with innate, inherent schemata and the earliest experiences, to which further experiences are then aligned. Previously developed cognitive structures have the tendency to live on and to integrate new experiences in the existing organisational structures – in cognitive science this is described as the top-down process. Different experiences are aligned with each other through this processing and then fall into the same category. This process of alignment is simply a feature of self-organising systems. This means, interestingly, that Jung's theory of complexes is supported by modern cognitive sciences (see Roesler & van Uffelen 2018). As was detailed above, it is still questionable that the brain's design is actually so similar from person to person, as is assumed here. Rather, different earlier experiences lead to strong differences even in the physiology of the central nervous system (see Bauer 2002).

Cognitive developmental psychology assumes, in agreement with neuroscientific insights in neural development, that initially a maximum number of synaptic connections will be formed between the neurons in a child's brain in embryonic development and in the first few months of life. Depending on their activation, these synaptic connections will be strengthened or atrophy through a lack of use (Kandel 2006). Interestingly, the Freudian authors Turnbull and Solms (2005) comment in relation to this that

we are all born with more synapses than we need. These synapses represent the potential connections between neurons that may be needed one day for the development of the inner map or model of the world within which we are operating. In a certain sense they represent all possible worlds in which we could possibly find ourselves. The actual environment that we are born into means that only a part of these connections is activated.

(p. 76)

We could read this as evidence for Jung's notion that archetypes are the underlying basis of all complexes which are based on individual experience.

The convergence principle could also be applied in principle in social communities, as the theory of social systems does, which also regards human communities as subject to the principle of self-organisation. In this sense it could be argued, as the ethnologist Claude Lévi-Strauss (1976) has already done in relation to the intercultural correspondence of social rules and rituals, that human communities all over the world and throughout history solve the same structural problems, for example, how to avoid conflict in the community, with the same social rules and processes, because these have been formed over generations as good Gestalts.

4.3.4 Archetypes as emerging structures

More recent Jungian authors see a solution to the dilemma described above first and foremost in the scientific concept of 'emergence' (Tresan 1996, Knox 2003, Hogenson 2004, summarised by Merchant 2012, p. 59ff). In emergent processes, connections of fundamental building blocks or the cooperation of elements of a system lead to qualitative leaps onto a whole new level, in which completely new regularities apply and which cannot be predicted from the features of the individual components. It is now argued that archetypes have no localisation, for example, in genes, but rather are wholly emergent phenomena: '[Archetypes are] the emergent characteristics of the developmental dynamic of the brain, the environment, and narrative' (Hogenson 2001, p. 27). Merchant (2009) summarises the argument as follows:

the possibility that there are no such things as pre-existent, innate archetypal structures which direct psychological life and which are at the core of complex development. Rather there would be developmentally produced mind/brain structures (image schemas) underpinning a later scaffolding through various processes of emergence and self-organisation. It is the latter which has the capacity to generate symbolic imagery. The crucial point is that such imagery would be arising out of mind brain structures which are themselves derived from early preverbal developmental experience and not from innate archetypes. The ramifications are substantial, for the very existence of archetypes as Jung conceived them is called into question.

(p. 342)

This line of thought in analytical psychology assumes, therefore, that archetypes, in the sense that Jung speaks about them, cannot be conceptualised in terms of genetic transmission. Instead, archetypal structures develop from an interaction between developmental experiences and the basic structure of the brain (Merchant 2006). Nevertheless, it is emphasised, this calls the universality of structures formed in this way into question because not all people have exactly the same experiences in their development. Jean Knox (2003), who can be considered the pre-eminent representative of the emergence position, has developed the theory of the fundamental schema or 'image pattern', which applies here. Image schemas, one of the principle concepts in cognitive semantics, are the first forms of representations formed in the child's brain by using the inherent capability of the brain as a complex, adaptive system for self-organisation and can therefore be seen as 'centres of attraction' (attractors) inside of the human self-organisation system (Hampe 2005). Based on current knowledge, genes can be seen to contain less specific information and instead contain predispositions for development which are then triggered if they come into contact with corresponding environmental stimuli. As far as mental development is concerned, the genes responsible for this apparently serve primarily to direct attention towards certain stimuli, thus enabling further neuronal stimulation and cortical development. As has been already mentioned, there is a genetically fixed behaviour pattern which brings newborn humans to fixate for longer on those structures which match human faces than on other objects. This would usually lead caregivers to interpret the infant's gaze as communication and to respond in turn with communication so that an interactive relationship is formed, which serves as a developmental environment for the baby and promotes its further cognitive maturation. Thus, the gene ensures a basic behavioural pattern with only a minimal amount of information. For differentiated structures to emerge from the interaction between pattern and environment in a process of emergence, however, the presence of certain qualities in the environment is required.

> Innate mechanisms focus the infant's attention onto features in the environment which are crucial to the infant's survival; these mechanisms are biologically based and have arisen through the process of natural selection because they improve chances of survival. Innate mechanisms are activated by environmental cues, interacting with them and organising them, leading to the formation of primitive spatial and conceptual representations (image schemas or archetypes). These form the foundation on which more complex representations can later be built.
>
> (Knox 2001, p. 631)

These 'primitive schemata or archetypes' are more or less universal, because the basic conditions of the environment on this level, on which the attention of the infant is directed, are the same all over the world and therefore the archetypes as 'image pattern' are 'reliably repeated early developmental achievements' (Knox 2004, p. 9).

But precisely this latter argumentation seems questionable: how can we be sure that the environmental conditions of infants at this level are the same everywhere? This argumentation is, however, essential for the thesis that archetypes are universal.

It must be conceded, at least by the emergence theorists, that the described system is susceptible to interference, namely when the caregiver does not correspond to the normally expected pattern of action because, for example, he or she is depressed and does not register the inherent interaction initiative in the infant's gaze. The basal pattern then does not lead to the development of a fostering environment or to the development of emergent structures. In turn, this means that if the basal pattern is inherent, the presence of emergent structures in all individuals cannot be assumed. They would, therefore, no longer be universal. At this point in the argument, therefore, it becomes apparent that archetypes are possibly conveyed through cultural transmission to a much greater extent than Jung had assumed.

4.3.5 *Mirror neurons and the 'intersubjective shared space'*

The existence of subliminal pathways, along which the knowledge of experience can be passed from generation to generation without this corresponding to a normal social interaction, is also possible. Neuroscientists have provided evidence for such a transference with the discovery of the so-called mirror neurons (Rizzolati et al. 2004, Gallese 2003, Bauer 2005). It was possible to show, in neurobiological studies, that specific mirror neuron systems exist for the perception of emotions and that we can as a result empathise with an observed emotion of another human.

> The system of mirror neurons may have had an especially significant function for the development of human beings and their cultures: a possible conservation and transfer of knowledge both inside of the same species and across generations [...] the mirror system and a kind of memory of humanity. In the hundred thousands of years before the invention of writing, books, and the internet, these stocks of knowledge were like living libraries which [...] could be passed onto one generation to the next through resonance and the learning of the model. Such a transfer was already possible at a time when language did not yet exist, because the resonance mechanism anchored in the mirror system

functions prelingually [...] because language describes ideas about processes and sequences that are stored as programs in the mirror neuron system.

(Bauer 2005, p. 168/169)

This sounds a lot like a neurobiological description of the collective unconscious. At a conference of the Italian Centre of Analytical Psychology in Milan in January 2009 Vezzoli 2009, Knox 2009, Jungians and neuroscientists discussed the applicability of the most recent results in brain research and cognitive developmental psychology for the archetype concept of Jungian psychology. In the summary, the hosts come to the following conclusion:

> This view assumes that complexes are formed in the process of primary interactions with the care-giver that are mainly bodily interactions involving mirror neurons. The primary interactions are internalised in the sense that the motor action chains become established patterns to be used and experienced in different goal directed actions that will later emerge as embodied concepts. In their development, complexes follow the same path. They start at birth with the process of integration and deintegration and are formed by the interaction of body and brain, but it is our creation of autobiographically based stories that gives significance and meaning to these social and physical interactions. [...] The hypothesis that is yet to be verified is that the body carries the memory of the interactions that form the complexes, that there are bodily reactions when an affective content is activated, and that narration is the transformation of embodied concepts into a functional meaning.
>
> (Vezzoli 2009, pp. 304–305)

The most interesting thing about this is that neuroscientists have evidently discovered inherent neural chains of command or concatenations of excitation patterns (Knox 2009, p. 310). Their hypothesis proposes that there are species-specific, preferred chains of action which can be reproduced more quickly across the mirror neurons of the young of a species, if they observe these in their fellow species. The foundation for acquiring these chains of action quickly is, according to the hypothesis, that the neural chains of command for these forms of action are already – dependent on genetics – engraved into the 'hardware' of the brain. Apart from the fact that this is here initially a hypothesis, this may in no way be used as a justification to speak of innate mental patterns or even ideas. Knox (2009, p. 311) once again explicitly implies

> that the fact that animals demonstrate patterns of automatic motor action, documented and researched by ethologists such as Lorenz and Tinbergen, is mistakenly used by Jungians as the basis for arguing archetypes are also an inherited pattern of mental representation, imagery and thought, apparently part of our genetic make-up, waiting to be activated by appropriate environmental cues. I suggested that this is a misunderstanding of the distinction between:
>
> a) automatic motor processes – the intentional action chains described by Fogassi et al. (2005) and
> b) mental representation, both conscious and unconscious.
>
> Automatic behavior patterns can be under significant genetic influence [...] mental imagery and thought are the result of much more complex interactions between brain, mind and environment, in which genetic 'hard-wiring' plays virtually no part.
>
> (author's emphasis)

This position argues something similar to the aforementioned attempt to explain the acquisition of universally homogeneous forms through interperson interaction and cultural tradition, possibly also in an unconscious way via resonance of the mirror neuron system. For Jungians, this means that they should be far more concerned with the social processes of the transfer of 'archetypal' patterns and along with this cultural and intercultural processes than with biology and genes. In particular, the transmission of identity-forming narrative patterns should be brought into focus here, as philosophers of consciousness (Hendricks-Jansen 1996) have long argued:

> If consciousness is the outcome of narratives that are not deliberately planned but that resemble the species-typical behavior of web-spinning spiders and dam-building beavers, shouldn't a study of consciousness begin by investigating these typically human activity patterns in their natural surroundings [...] Instead of trying to justify functional components and internal representations of a fully-fledged conscious mind by appeals to natural selection, wouldn't it be more logical to try to discover the underlying activity patterns that make it possible for a human infant to acquire this unique, unconscious ability to spin narratives about himself and the world? How exactly do narratives spin us? Or, to put it differently, how do our conscious selves become established as the result of participating in public dialogue that consists of coherent intentional stories.
>
> (p. 335)

4.3.6 A reformulation of the archetype concept

Based on this argument, the author (Roesler 2012a, 2012b) has made an attempt to formulate a coherent theory of archetypes, which is in line with our current knowledge of genetics, neurobiology, and developmental psychology. Different levels have been distinguished with regards to what we understand as archetypal.

1   **Inherent, Basal Schemas**: For newborn humans, there are in fact inherent, genetically fixed schemes of behaviour which produce a universally similar behaviour pattern. These schemes of behaviour are, however, extremely basic, something as primitive as reflexes. When the newborn child fixates for longer on structures which resemble human faces than on others, this does not mean that something

like an *idea* of the human face or another person is present. These basic schemas code no symbolic information at all and are far removed from those which Jung imaged as the archetypes. Moreover, the number of these inherent schemas is extremely limited, perhaps in the double figures, and can in this way never represent the variety of archetypal patterns in adults that Jung spoke of. Nevertheless, complex mental structures develop, as we have seen, out of these basic schemas through processes of emergence. The basic schemes are evolutionarily inherent, so that they can adjust the infant's behaviour to the genetic information with minimal effort and above all require a caregiver to behave correspondingly, so that the optimal conditions for the neural development of the child are created. An emergent processes area forms here through the cooperation of the inherent schemas with environmental factors. That also means, however, that the emergent structures are much more heavily dependent on interactive experiences, whose universal similarity is also in no way guaranteed, as Jung had originally thought.

2   **Prelinguistic   Representations   of   Experiences   of Relationships**: The inherent schemata are adjusted so that they 'require' the certain environmental conditions for which they are adapted. For the CONSPEC schema that would mean that the genetic predisposition requires the presence of an attachment figure who is emotionally targeted by the child's gaze and therefore interacts with the child and enters into a stable relationship with them. From this relationship and a whole series of similarly repetitive interactions, a more complex psychological structure can then develop in the infant, a kind of expectation: when I look at Mom, she talks to me, touches me, and so on. A sensual interaction develops and this is always the case. That could become the beginning of a mother complex, to which similar experiences would then be attached. In this sense, this complex could be described as archetypal, because the described process of a successful early relationship is, so to speak, 'conceived of by nature'. The genetic

predisposition of the inherent schemata senses nothing else; it aims at producing such a successful relationship and at the production of good mothering. Here, we could speak of an archetype of interaction or of dialogue, as Stadler (1997) has already claimed. As stated, the mental structures on this second level are no longer, however, universal, but rather interindividually different, because the process provided by nature is prone to disturbances. Under certain conditions (stress, mental disturbances, and so on) the caregiver may possibly not reliably react positively to the child's gaze and a different mental structure is created in the child through this.

It becomes clear, therefore, that on this second level inner representations form for the child based on continually repeating and similar experiences. These representations have been described in psychoanalysis as 'object relationships' and in infant research as 'representations of interactions that are generalized' (Stern 1985). Kast (1990) has worked out that these representations in a modern understanding can be equated with the complexes of analytical psychology. Stern (1985) makes it clear that these representations are created out of the interaction between an image of the Self and an image of the Other as well as from an accompanying feeling or an emotional tinge – what can be described in psychoanalytic terminology as a 'scenario'. These relationship and interaction representations play an essential role in therapy situations (Lichtenberg 1983) 'as model scenarios'. These exist on a prelinguistic and preconceptual level and can therefore only be restaged as forms of interaction. Neuroscientific findings on memory and its processing in cognitive psychological models provide an empirically based description of these prelinguistic representations (Knox 2001). The implicit memory is here described as a form of how previous experiences influence our perceptions, thoughts, and actions which exist fully outside of consciousness. This immediately suggests that this implicit memory can be regarded as a neural basis for unconscious complexes.

What can be called archetypal about it? It is evident that there is not an infinite number of variations of relationship patterns developed early on, as well as the resulting inner representations (which always also contain a processing or a contribution from the child). Instead, these can be arranged into a limited number of types, as has been done in empirical ways in attachment research (see Strauss et al. 2002), and these types of attachment – also intercultural types – can be replicated again and again in similar ways. The feature of universality would here, therefore, be fulfilled. The types of attachment should only serve as an example here for the categorisation of relationship patterns and relationship pathologies interindividually and interculturally into a limited number of types. Evidently, the 'design' of the human intellect and the human psyche work together here with the given conditions of human (co)existence and create certain typable forms. Now we have, on this second level, something like complex mental structures in the sense of expectations, therefore rudimentary ideas. These are, however, still very far from something so complex as the archetype of the hero myth, as Jung describes it.

3 **Cultural Patterns**: What Jung described as archetypal, and what is actually interesting for the practice of analytical psychology, are process patterns, for example, the individuation process, the therapeutic transformation, the myth of the hero, or aspects of these. They describe a process of transformation from a starting point, through different states of change and operations, to a final condition. As a rule, the starting point depicts something negative, a problematic situation, a deficiency, a disturbance, and this is transformed by the archetypal process into a state of solution. In principle, these process patterns can be transferred verbally and have the form of a narrative when regarded linguistically. The narrative presents a connection between the biologically determined basic schemata and the much more complex process pattern. We have seen that the basic schemata direct the infant's perception to the attachment

figure and the relationship pattern that is created, in other words the constantly repeating and similar relationship experiences that are reflected in representations. These representations describe processes of action between Self and Other, and change from a starting condition (e.g., fearful) to a final condition (secure and relaxed). In this regard, these earliest representations present early forms of narratives. It could be thought, then, that in the child there is a representation, in the sense of the second level, based on early experiences, which in their core correspond with an archetypal story pattern of the third level, and that the person, if they come into contact with the story, would 'recognise' it. An eight-year-old child can therefore feel as if the fairy tale of Hansel and Gretel speaks to them, because they carry in themselves a representation of an earlier abandonment experience, which is nevertheless preconceptual. That such parallels exist was impressively made clear by M. Gergen (1996) in a study of the context between central narratives and aspects of life stories. She asked college students about their favourite stories as children. In parallel, she collected the life stories, the self-images, and certain aspects of the current lives of participants in biographical interviews and was able to draw clear parallels with the patterns of the favourite stories of their respective childhoods. We must then assume that these early, usually prelinguistic, experiences are formed by a kind of primitive, metaphorical, and pictorial thought, in which a subjective experience is condensed into pictures and scenes, which we then call archetypal images. But how is it conceivable that a whole canon of archetypal process patterns can be found in an individual and that they can produce patterns which do not come from individual experience? As we have seen, these symbolic structures cannot be inherent. How do they, therefore, come to be in the individual?

The archetypal story/process patterns are passed on through cultural transmission in the course of socialisation as part of the cultural canon. There is also something like a predisposition, based on the prelinguistic representations of relationship experiences in connection with the archaic metaphoric thought mentioned above, to recognise and to absorb certain narrative patterns as archetypal patterns. My thesis here is that for the acquisition or learning of archetypal process patterns, something similar to Chomsky's (1978) previously mentioned 'language acquisition device' exists in the neural structure. My assumption here is that children and adolescents, both in similar ways, assimilate during the socialisation process the archetypal structures, with which they come into contact in the form of the cultural story canon, in an implicit way and store them in their implicit memory, through a pattern recognition system for archetypal 'patterns'. It is possible that this is made easier by the narrative or process patterns, which we define as archetypal, being similar to the structure of the prelinguistic representations of interactions. Here this would also mean that experience and socialisation play a bigger role in the acquisition of the archetypes than Jung had conceived. A possibility for the explanation of such a pattern recognition system for archetypal structures lies in the mirror neuron system mentioned above.

> Because this mechanism is typical of all humans, the system of the mirror neurons *represents a supra-individual neural format, through which a shared inter-human space* is created. Because the content of this shared human semantic space *contains programs for all typical, experience related occurring sequences of behavior and feeling inside of their own species*, it also forms the intuitive basis for the feeling of a – by and large – calculable, predictable world.
>
> (Bauer 2005, p. 166/167; my emphasis)

The programs of reactions, which everyone keeps available for typically occurring situations, can be activated, harmonized, and communicated by resonance from person to person. Mirror nerve cells have then settled themselves in the brain, where programs for sequences of action and associated sensations are stored [...] the mirror neurons represent in this way a form of social neurobiological format, they are the common multiple which is found in every individual, but also in the community.

(Ibid., p. 159)

In almost the same words, the neuroscientist Vittorio Gallese (2003) speaks of the 'shared meaningful intersubjective space'.

The archetypes and the collective unconscious would not be in individuals' biological make-up, but based rather in interpersonal exchange and are therefore social phenomena. The shared archetypal structures would be acquired, therefore, in a long process of unconscious exchange of experiences and programmes of behaviour intuitive mimicry and resonance, which requires socialisation. In this sense, the memory of humanity, of the collective, is passed on. The question here is not whether the transference is biological or cultural. It is both, a neurobiologically based sociocultural transference of the deepest kind.

In light of these insights, it seems to me to be central that Jung's conception of archetypes as genetically inherent must ultimately be relinquished. Other ways of transference can, however, at least hypothetically, be constructed. It should also be clear that socialisation plays a considerable role in this and that it can proceed in many different ways and calls into question the universality of all archetypes. On the other hand, we should also not underestimate the immense influence that enculturation, this being an upbringing in a distinct culture, has on the development of the mind, in particular the unconscious part. Jung himself even once expressed that: 'Culture is a part of our nature'. Every culture provides narrative patterns for typical, shared human experiences. This is how cultural archetypes are created. A person is not born with a collective unconscious, but rather he grows into it during the course of socialisation, and in this regard is the collective unconscious a cultural unconscious, as has been formulated by Joseph Henderson (1991). This view also implies, however, that a theory of archetypes must be much more concerned with the humanities and cultural studies and no longer with the question of genetics, of behavioural biology, or the search for universals. Moreover, it would be interesting to investigate in detail the development of an archetypal pattern in the socialisation process.

4.4 Research on the collective unconscious, in the sense of an unconscious, interpersonal connection

The explanations so far also relate of course to the hypothesis of a collective unconscious, although so far rather in the sense of the content of the unconscious, namely the archetypes. In what follows, research and concepts which relate to the second aspect of Jung's conception of this hypothesis shall be presented, more specifically that of an unconscious connection between different people and groups. Jung assumed that a shared unconscious space forms between analyst and client, in particular in the process of analysis, which could be described in analytical psychology today as an 'interactive sphere', in which processes of unconscious exchange and transfer take place. Totally unlike the concept of archetypes, these unconscious interaction processes have long been the research object of psychoanalysis in the Freudian tradition (e.g., Baranger & Baranger 2009; Buchholz 2005).

With regards to a systematic investigation of unconscious exchange processes of this kind, attention should be drawn to two research groups. First, that of Rainer Krause at the University of Saarbrücken as well as the Boston infant researchers working with the psychoanalyst Daniel Stern. Krause researched over many years the unconscious, emotive transference process between two people having a conversation with the Differential Affect Scale (DAS; Krause 2010). As part of this, people were recorded on video in conversation and the images of their faces were projected onto a split screen. The facial expressions, and therefore the connected emotions, of the people could then be coded with the DAS. Through this it can be shown that the more strongly the one person is mentally troubled, the more the coding of the facial expressions of the other person matches that of the patient. This is systematic proof of an unconscious synchronisation of emotional exchange. Krause provided empirical evidence for emotional transference and countertransference processes.

Infant research has also been intensely concerned in the last decades with the unconscious exchange process between the infant and the caregiver, an example of which can be found in the work of Stern and his colleagues in the Boston Process of Change Study Group. This study also revolved around the microanalysis of interaction processes which were recorded on video. A key finding is that at the beginning of its life a child is already existentially dependent on a relationship, which consists of a common mental world and in which synchronisation and resonance take place. In principle, this research has not only confirmed Rene Spitz's (1965) concept of the coenesthetic perception but also expanded it. The researchers in Boston talk about a system of 'relational psychophysiology' (Tronick 1998), by which they suggest that numerous physiological processes like endocrinology, the immune system, and the circadian rhythm of the infant are coordinated with the physiological processes of the mother. This close mental and physiological interrelationship between the mother and the child is created by rhythmic synchronisation in their interaction, for example, in relationship to head movements, eye contact, voice modulation, phonetic speaking, and others. This deeply unconscious exchange that reaches into the physical world between both people is, however, not only limited to early childhood, but can even be found in adults. It was demonstrated in a study that masculine and feminine test subjects could tell from voice alone the most fertile days of a speaker's female cycle (Gödde & Buchholz 2011). The synchronisation of the menstrual cycle between women in one family or even between good friends could be proved. All of this confirms Jung's hypothesis of an unconscious connection or a coalescence between humans, which he described with the term 'participation mystique', which he borrowed from French anthropology.

While the mental synchronisation process between people having a conversation or communicating in some other way can be explained to some degree, this becomes more difficult for the latter phenomena, although it can be assumed that the exchange of sensory perceptions still takes place (e.g., smells). This becomes, however, fully inexplicable when the people involved have no physical contact with each other and thus no contact takes place that is perceivable through sensory organs. Different neuroscientific studies have attempt to shed light on which neuropsychological mechanisms lie behind this phenomenon of synchronisation over distance. A research group at Princeton University were able to prove with imaging processes that a synchronisation of neural excitation patterns occurs between two people, which the authors describe as neural coupling (Stephens et al., 2010). What is most interesting about this is that this neural coupling/synchronisation only comes into being if both people sympathise with each other. In a similar German study, the same could be proved with the EEG research tool: a direct transfer of event-related potentials (ERPs) in the EEG takes place between the two people, in particular if they, for example, are connected through previous shared meditation (Seiter 2003). A virtually telepathic connection in the brains could even be proved in EEG studies (Hinterberger & Anton 2012). Correlations in the alpha bands were found in subjects who were up to 750km apart from one another.

To explain such phenomena, the so-called generalised quantum theory, which arose as a result of the further development of quantum physics and the dialogue between Jung and Pauli, was developed (Atmannspacher et al. 1995). It is common knowledge that Jung discussed with the quantum physicist and Nobel Prize winner Wolfgang Pauli his concept of synchronicity or the Unus Mundus. Jung's hypothesis was that the division of the empirically tangible world into mental phenomena on the one hand and physical phenomena on the other hand (the so-called Cartesian dualism) stood facing a world in which, although the phenomena only exist as potential and are not manifested, a separation has not yet occurred, but rather in this Unus Mundus mental and physical are still connected. Pauli and Jung compared this to the observances of the double nature of light. Depending on the experimental set-up, light can be either a wave or a particle, which contradicts classical physics. Quantum physics assumes that light represents only potential before it is measured, and the observance/measurement/perception only then determines what it manifests itself as. The quantum world is characterised by certain features which contradict classical physics. Here non-locality (the location of a particle is only to a certain extent approximately determinable) or entanglement (spatially separated particles can nevertheless directly interact) applies and there is no continual flow of time as well as no conventional causality. Jung and Pauli imagined the Unus Mundus and the collective unconscious analogously. This Unus Mundus as a potential sphere is structured by the archetypes, the imperceptible orders of phenomena, which in turn only manifest in the classical world either as psychic or physical phenomena (Atmanspacher et al. 2002, Roesler 2014). The basic idea is that all human reality constructs itself on quantum phenomena because these particles are the foundations of the whole physical and neural reality. If, however, non-locality, timelessness, or simultaneity, and a causality, as well as entanglement, dominate in the quantum world, that must also have an impact on human reality. For our investigation that means that the archetypes as intangible structuring principles exist in a sphere of potentiality and manifest themselves during the transition via the so-called Heisenberg cut either as a physical phenomenon or as a psychospiritual one. Synchronistic phenomena suggest, however, that they manifest themselves in both spheres synchronously. This sphere of potential can also bridge the gap between physical and mental in the world that can be experienced. It is, therefore, possible to imagine that mental content, at least as potentialities, transfer themselves across this sphere from one defined individual to another or that we all participate in this potential space (see also Roesler 2015). This would defend a theory of the acquisition of mental archetypes because they always exist as potentialities and all individuals participate in that. Incidentally, this variant of the explanation of the emergence of archetypes, which corresponds to Jung's above-mentioned 'transcendental argument', is theoretically the most coherent.

5 Applications of the archetype theory

From the very beginning, archetype theory was above all a clinically applied concept. Jung developed his archetype theory while working at the psychiatric clinic at the University in Zürich in order to explain the bizarre and partly archaic contents of the fantasies and hallucinations of his psychotic patients. This approach, which Jung first applied together with Eugen Bleuler, was revolutionary because he attributed a meaning to the contents of the hallucinations. In this way, Jung was able to observe that patients who were approaching the outbreak of a psychosis regularly painted pictures with those motifs, which Jung later described as mandalas. Jung saw in this choice of image the attempt to orient and to centre the psyche, which was threatening to collapse, into an ordered structure. Alongside the clinical usage, however, archetype theory has always been a cultural theory. Even today, it serves the purpose of explaining cultural phenomena as well as typical motifs in art, in narratives, and in other forms.

One of Jung's central assumptions here is that archetypes in symbolic form appear and first feature as images. The image is for Jung the primary form of expression of the unconscious psyche, or the connection between the unconscious and consciousness. This does not completely correspond with today's understanding of developmental psychology, which assumes that the first representations are embodiments, schemata of action. All cognitive development theories after Jean Piaget assume that the first mental representations of a small child are

DOI: 10.4324/9781003058458-5

sensomotoric schemata and that the first representations are enactive and not iconic. Modern psychoanalysis takes this into account insofar as that it assumes that the central unconscious conflict is not linguistically representable, but is rather enacted in the therapeutic relationship, to which the analyst in turn reacts with the so-called scenic understanding and so tries to decipher a message from the enactment. In the field of analytical psychology today, connections to this new perspective can also be found, for example, in Jungian Peter Schellenbaum's (1995) approach to developing so-called spontaneous rituals from the spontaneous gestures of the client, which in psychotherapy can point the way to the resolution of conflict situations, or in other words an approach that remains on the level of action dialogue. For the classic approach in Jungian psychology, however, the image is primary and always prevailing. From this, the extensive methods of working with symbolic material have developed, alongside the work with images and the sandplay, in particular the interpretation of dreams, which are further exemplified below. First, however, Jung's basic methods of approaching the meaning of archetypes, what can be referred to as amplification, should be explained.

5.1 The amplification method

To identify the archetypal meaning of symbols, images, or mythical forms in a systematic way, Jung developed an original method: amplification. Literally translated this means an encircling or going around the symbol. The concrete practice involves initially the collection of specific symbols and their meaning in different cultures, time periods, religions, mythologies, and so on. The parallel, overlapping meanings here are predominantly of interest. The process of encircling the symbol also means, however, that normally not just one clear meaning is specified, but instead a network of meanings is created with the specific symbol at its centre. From a depth psychological perspective, it can be said that the use of this specific symbol sets the whole network into motion. In concrete cases the task is then to find out which aspect of this network of meanings is being addressed. This approach coincides with the neuroscientific understanding of early psychoanalysis and psychiatry in general in Jung's time, which had been predominantly interested in associationism. Here it is assumed that elements of meaning in the brain are connected with each other through associative paths. Freud, therefore, also chose his method of free association in order to finally reach the core of the conflict from one meaningful element to another. Interestingly, this notion has been confirmed in recent neuroscientific research, which states that meaning in the brain is not located in certain places (localisationism), but instead is rooted in networks which are synchronously activated (connectionism): 'what fires together, wires together'.

In the application of the amplification method, as many parallel uses of a specific symbol in different cultural contexts as possible are collected. For this purpose, the use of certain symbol lexica and other resources has become established in analytical psychology. Analytical psychology refuses to use lexicons of symbols that assign a clear meaning to a symbol (e.g., the tower to mean phallus) because of the background presented above. Instead, those symbol lexica which give an overview of different applications of the symbol in different cultural contexts are used. Some recommended examples are:

> *An Illustrated Encyclopaedia of Traditional Symbols* by Cooper (1986), *Herder Symbol Dictionary* (Österreicher-Mollwo 1990), *Dictionary of German Superstition* (Bächtold-Stäubli 2000), the collection *Man and His Symbols* (Jung et al. 1968); symbolism of plants (Brosse 1992), of trees (Brosse 1994), and of animals (Zerling & Bauer 2003); symbolism of basic patterns (Riedel 1985a); symbolism of colours (Riedel 1985b); number symbolism (Betz 1989).

A more recent, comprehensive representation and interpretation of archetypal symbols comes from the authors of the *Archive of Research in Archetypal Symbolism* (ARAS) (2011) at the Jung Institute in Los Angeles. ARAS also has an excellent website available, on which over 17,000 depictions of symbols are stored and can be specifically searched for. Along with these, there are numerous articles and essays on individual symbols, images, and archetypal representations (www.aras.org).

Finally, Jung's collected works can be used as a huge source of symbolic meaning. Jung was concerned for the most part of his life with studying the meaning of archetypes and pursuing them in different cultural and religious contexts. It is possible to do so, as there is a detailed index of the complete collected works in which the corresponding text passages for numerous keywords and symbols can be found. (A practical example of an amplification of a symbol from a dream series can be found in Chapter 5.3.2).

5.2 Clinical application

5.2.1 Character – identity – biography

A very early idea connected to Jung's archetype concept was to assume that the unique core of a human's personality, their being, is archetypally determined. This idea can be found again in the later formulation of the archetype of the Self, which contains the individuality of the person, but which likewise – paradoxically – encompasses the entirety of the person. The idea here is that in every human, a certain essential core is archetypal, meaning preformed and inherent, which wants to find expression and to be lived. James Hillmann (2002) took this concept further, to its most radical conception, in his book *The Soul's Code*. Here he argues that in every person, the individuality of the personality, and by extension essentially their path through life, has been embryonically predetermined before birth and this nature will assert itself against all obstacles in life. He puts forward in detail numerous examples from human history, of personalities from politics, arts, and so on. Jung also had the idea that, during an inner conflict, if a person plots their life path against this preformed personality core, it can lead to a mental disorder. The critical question in the framework of a Jungian psychoanalysis would be, then, which archetype or which myth this person should actually live out, because only this will lead to meaning in their own life. Jung, however, takes issue with the fact that an overwhelming identification with an archetype in day-to-day life can be seen as pathological; he even created a clinical term for this, namely that of 'inflation'. Inflation would be an overwhelming identification, or even a conflation with a particular archetype, or the archetypal image flooding out of the collective unconscious into consciousness, so that consciousness drowns, metaphorically speaking, in the archetype. It no longer has any room for decision, so to speak, but is controlled by the archetypal pattern of action.

Case Study: A man of about 40 came despairingly to psychotherapy because he had a series of failed relationships with women in his past. At the beginning of these there had been a lot of love, but the estrangement between the partners had increased and finally the women had ended the relationships, without the man being able to understand why this had happened. In the biographical case history it was clear that the client had had a very tense relationship with his parents, characterized by violence. There was a tendency for the father to violently abuse the mother, and the boy felt loyally connected to the mother as a victim and attempted to protect her from the violent father. In adolescence, as the client was able to stand up to the father, he effectively managed to shelter the mother from the father's abuse. In his own early relationships, it became apparent that he had developed a strong unconscious identification with the image of the heroic liberator of persecuted women and the saviour of the victim, and this pattern was repeated unconsciously in every new relationship. Of course his own needs in the relationship fell completely by the wayside, and the partners became increasingly less enthusiastic as the relationship went on and felt increasingly oppressed and demanded of, which regularly led then to the end of the relationship.

Both concepts, the identification with the archetype as inflation as well as the working out of the archetypal essence, can be considered as an increased orientation towards archetypal basic patterns, which serves to reorient or centre the personality in the face of the challenge or crisis, most notably during critical events or processes. The author has personally investigated this concept in an empirical study (Roesler 2006). Biographical interviews were conducted with 20 people who had faced a chronic illness or a disability in the course of their life and had to process this intrusion into their former identity. The idea behind this was that in a situation where one's former identity is questioned, due to the intrusion of an illness or disability, the identity must be reconstituted and archetypal structures can have a stronger impact, which then shape the identity. It was possible to show that particularly those who had successfully overcome the crisis in their lives relied very heavily on concise archetypal storytelling patterns when designing their life stories. Moreover, this resulted in a limited list of different archetypal patterns in the biographies which different participants selected, independently from each other, for the reconstruction of their identity.

As an example of the results of the investigation, the archetype of religious conversion or conversion narrative will now be described more fully. Three biographies from the study place a religious conversion at the centre of the construction of their identity and their processing of the questions that the illness or disability posed for their lives. Conversion means a sudden and dramatic event, which is irrational in nature. It contains the appearance of a powerful, transpersonal power and depicts a unique event, which brings with it the negation of the old self and the affirmation of a new self, and the means change from a static condition to another, also static condition. Overall it represents a 'good thing' and a change in behaviour follows the change in belief. The shaping of one's own life story as conversion, at least with regard to analytical psychology, is based on an archetype of human life, a fundamental transformation of life through conversion. The most notable prototype of this archetypal life story pattern in our culture is the conversion of Saul to Paul as depicted in the New Testament book of Acts. In other religious and cultural circles, other comparable prototypical stories exist, for example, the conversion of the Indian emperor Ashoka to Buddhism. This intercultural dissemination proves the archetypal nature of this narrative pattern.

Table 5.1 Typology of the identified archetypal story patterns

Archetypal Narrative Pattern	Structural Elements	Specific narrative elements and strategies	Prototypical examples
Conversion/ Religious conversion	- Passage from old to new identity - Fundamental transformation from a previous, sinful life to a new, true life through God's power - Revaluation of all previous value - Membership of selected community - Missionary stimulus	- Authentication strategies for proof of transcendental effectiveness - Parallelisation of personal history with religious salvation stories - Use of predefined story formats of the religious community	The Damascene conversion in the narrative of the Apostles
Hero Mythology	- Life story as a fight against an opponent (illness, society, or similar), which seems hopeless because opponents are overpowering - Narrator is on his own ('exposed'), but also finds helpful characters - Identity itself worked out against resistance and crises, as a subjective achievement; concept of personal strength - Autonomy is of central importance - Narrator has a mission or message for the group - The fight is for a good cause and the opponent is evil	- Narrative contrasts/ oppositions (good–evil; helper–opponent) - Construction of ideal 'role model' persons as a guideline for own identity design	Classical hero sagas, for example, Siegfried, Perseus, Heracles

Table 5.1 Cont.

Archetypal Narrative Pattern	Structural Elements	Specific narrative elements and strategies	Prototypical examples
Psychotherapy as 'a new mythology' of self-realisation	A psychological interpretation of life: - Personality as a result of childhood experiences - Illness as psychosomatic - Life as a development process, as a progressive realisation of one's own self - Identity changing through psychotherapy - Use of psychological knowledge bases	- Use of the format 'self-actualisation narrative': progressive macro structure - 'Biographization' of the life story: high degree of self-interpretation of the life story - High degree of coherence	
Miraculous Healing Story	- Design as numinous event - Use of the motif of descent or death and rebirth for the experience of the disease - Listing of witnesses for proof of the miracle - Self-portrayal as healed despite permanent disability	- Authentication strategies: Witnesses to the miracle are presented in direct speech - Dramatisation through contrasts	Healing stories on votive tablets in shrines
Progress Mythology: Overcoming all illnesses through technical progress	- Overcoming the disease through technological progress - Narrator is part of a collective movement to overcome all the problems of humanity	- Change in narrative style marks technical overcoming of the disease - Emphasis on collective developments - Narrative concepts for the future	Pygmalion, Daedalus, Icarus,

Archetype of the Tragic Life	- Life story as progressive descent - Intertwining of one's own guilt and not being able to act differently, of ignorance, and not wanting to know - Illness as atonement for own mistakes - Results in greater wisdom	- Consistently regressive narrative format - Permanent changing of self-interpretations (e.g., error–ignorance) - Justification figures	Ancient tragedies, for example, Oedipus
Mythology of the innocent victim	- The narrative descent is indebted to others - Own identity is presented as unbroken	- Regressive narrative format - Constructed elaborately to make others experience guilt	Job
Narratives of discrimination/ the unjustly persecuted	- Illness as damage to social identity - Fear of stigmatisation as the dominant pattern of interpretation - Social others are seen as a potential threat - Life in hiding - Secrecy and unconditional adaptation/ normality as a life-determining principle	- Normalisation strategies	

Explaining one's own life story as a story of conversion is thus a form of processing and giving meaning to the experience of illness or disability, which is based on archetypal elements of meaning. By considering the three biographies comparatively, the following general structural features and characteristic narrative building blocks of this type of identity construction can be abstracted:

1   The conversion can be described as a passage from an old to a new identity, and therefore the experience of conversion splits the life into two sections, each of which contains very different significance and value and can be contrasted with the other. The narrator is given the status of a chosen one or initiated with this portrayal.

2   The person is fundamentally changed through the conversion, has acquired a fully new identity, which releases him to the Good, Right, True, and so on, thus conferring a profound meaning and uncovering all aspects of life.

3   This fundamental change is no biographical achievement, but rather relates back to the appearances of god or another unspecified superhuman, transcendental power.

4   The old life is treated either as fully inessential or reinterpreted based on the new self-interpretation after the conversion.

5   In this way, the earlier orientation in life is interpreted as somehow wrong, as an error, or as only a fragile self-certainty and negatively valued, while the new life is seen as correct, liberated, in line with a knowledge of the truth, or as a realisation of the true self and is therefore positively valued.

6   The conversion is accompanied by a complete re-evaluation and reversal of all previous values.

7   From the conversion experience, a missionary impulse or motivation develops, meaning the need to somehow pass on this personally experienced salvation or to pass on a message.

8   The conversion results in the taking up of and the indissoluble membership in a new religious community, which corresponds with religious truth.

9   In comparison to other biographies, there are a remarkable number of written records that detail this process, especially records which relate specifically to religion or other canons. This acts as evidence to refute potential doubters, who could call the conversion into question and who are evidently also a part of this archetypal pattern.

It can be empirically shown that in comparison with the other cases, the conversion archetype has particularly effectively contributed to a reconstruction of damaged or destroyed identities. An exemplary case from this investigation would be the narrative of Mr Quandt's life. Mr Quandt was largely paralysed as a result of a stroke and subsequently lost his ability to work, most of his bodily functions, his circle of friends, and finally also his marriage. In principle, therefore, his existence had been completely destroyed. After a difficult personal crisis, he finds a foothold in his personal belief, which brings about a comprehensive transformation towards a happier life which he had not known before his illness. In his depiction of this, the transformation is caused by the disability and the losses and suffering that came from this. It is precisely through the experience of having lost so much that all the things that remain, and even the few things that return, become immensely valuable and meaningful. Furthermore, the worthlessness of lots of things that he previously could not bear to lose becomes apparent. He exemplifies this in his marriage and friendships, which ended after his stroke, and prove themselves in this way as being ultimately not valuable. His transformation also brings him something new of value. He gains an understanding of marginalised groups and outsiders because he too has gotten to know pain, loss, and social rejection. The narrative of Mr Quandt follows the central Christian topos of development and transformation narratives from suffering to salvation. He explicitly compares his self-interpretation with the Christian salvation narrative:

1   I think I even developed a certain naivety through my faith,
     like by just saying 'we must'. And who has to can be quite
     naive about what support the gospel gives, it doesn't have
5   to be that much at all / [...] It's not just a big statement for
     me – the Lord is my shepherd. And then when things are
     going badly, I simply always felt that from the beginning,
     even in sickness, and I believed that it wouldn't be so bad
     for me, that it would never go so badly, that I would just get
     to the end. There is this wonderful story where, where the
     man who is at the end of his life meets Jesus, says I have had
10   so many phases where I was just alone in life or where you
     were not there Lord, and the Lord then says, that's just what
     you think and, and he sees his tracks through the life of
     the man, and sees then, whenever the very bad phases were
     he sees two tracks, Jesus says to him, you see that I have
     carried you there. No. Wrong, I miscounted, he actually
     sees / he always sees two tracks, and then when the he was
     in the really hard phases of life, when it was tough for him,
     he sees only one track, and then he says he sees Lord when
15   it was bad for me, I was alone there, he says. Jesus says no,
     I carried you.
     (Mr Quandt, Transcript 1)

The central aspect of all the stories told, which relate to meaning being constructed through religion, is that the religious canon provides stories for people which describe how humans find the actual meaning in their lives only through the influence or intervention of a transcendental power. A possible, but not necessary, aspect of interpretation is that this influence or intervention occurs only as a result of a situation in which the person is exposed, a situation of suffering, of the destruction of the former self-certainty.

Using the archetypal conversion narrative to shape one's own life provides a great deal of coherence and meaningfulness, because ultimately all life events, even those which are painful such as accidents, illness, and permanent disability, can be understood as part of a comprehensive, higher plan for life. In this way, it can be said that this (life) narrative archetype of one's own biographical experience of identity can confer to a particular degree wholeness and complete meaning.

5.2.2 The role of archetypes in the psychotherapeutic process

As we have already seen, mental disorders can be understood as a person being controlled by an archetype and this archetype is being staged in the person's life (inflation). Thus, it is in such a case important that in psychotherapy the archetype operating in the background is identified and the patient is made conscious of it, so that it can be differentiated from the Ego complex (Eschenbach 1986). On the other hand, psychotherapy can also revolve around recognising in the unconscious the archetypal essence of the person in the sense of their individuality, which has been missing so far in life. Laying this essence out in the open enables the person to consciously reorient themselves around this guideline as part of a genuine individuation process. This comparison makes it clear that Jung's psychotherapy essentially entails support on the path to individuation, which has been blocked or interrupted by problems in socialisation or in other phases of life and has led to a split between the direction of the conscious Ego and the unconscious essence, and thus the Self. Likewise, it is clear that the psychotherapeutic support of the individuation process represents a perpetual balancing act between two extremes. On one side, the overwhelming identification with a perhaps essentially foreign archetype, and on the other side, losing contact to one's own essence. The central method of navigating between the two poles is the conscious realisation of the archetypal material. That makes it possible for the client on the one hand to discern the archetypal contents and to delineate his or her personal Ego and his or her defined personality from these unconscious powers. On the other hand, he or she can now recognise his or her own essential nature by acknowledging the archetypal contents, which arise in his or her own consciousness, and allowing these parts of the personality an appropriate place in life. The complexity of this realisation process, which contains both separation and connection, was summarised after Jung in Erich Neumann's (1968) concept of the 'Ego-Self axis'. The psychotherapeutic process should help in this sense to reconnect the Ego with the Self so that the Ego is constantly built out of and nourished by the Self and also to strengthen the Ego enough that it can differentiate itself from the Self and not be consumed by it – the latter would amount to a psychosis.

How do archetypes express themselves concretely as part of a mental disorder or in the psychotherapeutic process? Several different levels can be differentiated from one another here:

1   According to the developmental psychology concept mentioned above, the basic level of expression of the archetypes is the unconscious acting out of an archetype in a person's actions. Archetypal patterns can also be seen in the bodily expressions of the symptoms of the mental disorder. So we can understand an addiction, for example, as an expression of the fact that the person had to painfully miss being carried by their mother ('holding') and the huge feeling of coalescence that comes along with this, and therefore as an adult still tries to reach this desired condition (with help of the addictive substance) without being able ultimately to internalise it. Another example would be a person with obsessive compulsive disorder who must always, in endless repetition, wash their hands due to the deep guilt feeling connected with their own aggressive impulses, without this ever giving them relief from the feeling of guilt.

2   The next level of differentiation on which archetypal patterns can appear is represented through images. These most notably spontaneously appear in dreams. Typical examples for this would be a recurring nightmare in whose image the central problem of the client is almost prototypically summarised. A client can, for example, dream of being about to take a critical exam, in which he then says something wrong, dodges a question, and the examiner rejects and fails him. Because the unconscious content, and also the archetypal content, is communicated above all through dreams, the therapeutic work with dreams and their interpretation still represent the key path to making the unconscious conscious in analytical psychology. Archetypal

images can also occur in daydreams, visions, ideas, and other imaginal phenomena. Moreover, in analytical psychology a pointed attempt is made to offer the unconscious a stage, in order to bring about archetypal images by requesting that the client paint images or take part in therapeutic sand play and create sand pictures (Riedel 1985b). In this way it is possible to receive a pictorial representation of the archetypal contents, which makes interpretation and processing possible. It can frequently be observed in the therapeutic process that clients spontaneously grasp on to this medium of picture drawing in order to express the contents with which they are most deeply concerned inside. In Jungian understanding, just the formation of an image is an essential step in the confrontation with the archetypal material and in this way is part of the means of making this material conscious.

3   Finally, however, this archetypal content needs to be brought onto a cognitive level in order to become conscious of the conflict. This happens most of all in verbal expression, by the inner experiences being related to the psychotherapist as part of the psychotherapy or by writing down the contents, as Jung himself had done in his confrontation with his unconscious in the form of the so-called Red Book.

So far, the depiction matches the classic approach in Jungian psychology. If both the publications in analytical psychology on working with archetypal material in the psychotherapeutic process, and the training practice at institutes are considered, the essential meaning of archetypes in the psychotherapeutic process lies only in the fact that their emergence as part of the psychotherapy presents a helpful construct stimulus which can put the clients on the right path towards integrating conflicts, towards healing and becoming whole. Formulated in a modern way, this use of archetypal stimuli in the psychotherapeutic process is a resource-oriented approach, which relies on the self-regulating and self-healing powers of the psyche. In this sense, archetypal elements represent information from the

unconscious which was not previously available to consciousness and are there to set in motion or support the process of
self-healing. In this way the archetype concept absolutely has
key significance for the psychotherapeutic process in analytical psychology. It can be assumed that universally present
archetypes become efficacious in crisis situations or during
periods of mental disturbance and express themselves in
dreams and symbolic material, supported by the therapeutic
framework and the relationship, and can initiate or structure
the healing process in the individual psyche. The framework
and the analytical relationship are almost precisely constructed
to set this process in motion and to support it. An example
that makes this relationship clear, can be found in the Tavistock
lectures (Jung CW 7) mentioned above, in which Jung refers
to the dream of a patient in which a crab appears, which Jung
interprets as information from the unconscious that the cere-
brospinal and sympathetic nervous system of the dreamer is
rebelling against his conscious attitude because a crab only has
this kind of nervous system. The client's unconscious created
a reference using the archetypal symbol to a body of knowledge which was not consciously accessible to the dreamer.
In this way the archetypal element transported an additional
piece of information, one which transcended the perspective
of consciousness ('transcendent function') and which aimed to
heal the patient and could be used in the therapeutic process.
That is the reason why in Jungian psychotherapeutic training
such an emphasis is put on knowledge of mythology and the
history of symbols. The therapist should be in a position to
recognise archetypal patterns in the dreams and symbolic
productions of the client. A further example for the application of the archetype concept in psychotherapy is the situation
presented in the Introduction to this book, in which the client
dreams of an initiation ritual and the unconscious hints at
the need for just such a transformation process for the client,
thereby informing the way in which the psychotherapy can
proceed. The dream provides, with its archetypal information,
indications for how the therapy should advance, for example,
that he should make a sacrifice. Dreams, fantasies, images,

and other symbolic material match an archetypal pattern, for example. a mythological narrative, and this provides information about the further development necessary for the personality, the advancement of the therapy, and so on. The Jungian scholar Marie-Louise von Franz makes this application of the archetype concept clear in numerous examples in her books about fairy tales (e.g., von Franz 1986). At the beginning of such a psychotherapy it would be standard to ask about the patient's favourite stories or favourite childhood fairy tales. It is assumed that in the emotional attraction or fascination to a particular story, it is possible to see a deep truth about the person's development. Psychologically speaking, the knowledge of a favourite story can contain indications of the path of development to be taken in therapy or significant insights into the nature of the person.

One of the leading examples of this approach can be found in Katrin Asper's book *Abandonment and Self-Alienation* (1989) in which she uses and interprets 'The Seven Ravens' from Grimm's book of fairy tales in order to describe the psychodynamics of a narcissistic disorder as well as the elements which are necessary to heal such a disorder in psychotherapy. The following passage comes from the original version (Asper 1989, p. 117f):

Once upon a time there was a mother who had three sons who played cards during church one Sunday. When the sermon was over, the mother came home and saw what they had done. She began cursing her godless children and suddenly they turned into coal-black ravens and flew up and away out of the house. The three brothers had, however, a little sister who loved them with all her heart and was so saddened by their banishment that she finally decided to go and look for them. She took nothing with her on the long, long journey aside from a little stool, which she would sit on when she became too tired, and ate nothing the whole time apart from wild apples and pears. But she could never find the three ravens, except once when they flew away over her head and dropped a ring. She picked this up and the little sister saw that it was the ring that she had once given to the youngest brother. But she kept on going, so wide, so far, until she came to the end of the world and she went to the sun, but it was far too hot and it ate little children. Then she came to the moon, but he was far too cold and also evil and when he saw her he said 'I smell human flesh'. That made her carry on going and she came to the stars, which were good to her and all sat on chairs and the morning star stood up and gave her a little chicken leg and said 'if you don't have the leg, then you can't get into the glass mountain and in the glass mountain you'll find your brothers'. The little girl took the chicken leg and wrapped it tightly in some cloth and went on until she came to the glass mountain. But the gate was locked. She went to get the chicken leg and hold it up, but she had lost it on her journey. Because she didn't know what to do and because she hadn't found any key at all, she took a knife and cut off her little finger and put it in the gate and happily unlocked it. A little dwarf came up to her and said: My child, what are you looking for here? I'm looking for my brothers, the three ravens. The Ravens are not here, said the dwarf, but do you want to wait inside? So she went in and the dwarf brought three plates and three glasses and the little sister ate a little from each plate and drank a little from each glass and dropped the ring in the last glass. All at once, there was a whirring and buzzing in the air and the dwarf said: The Ravens have come home. And the ravens all began to speak at once: Who has eaten from my plate? Who has drunk from my glass? As the third raven, however, came to his glass he found the ring there and realized that the little sister had arrived. They all recognized the ring and were all released again from the spell and went happily home.

The fairy tale makes clear in its symbols and images both the emergence and the problems of a narcissistically wounded personality and its depression, as well as providing the basic archetypal structure of healing and in this way almost a road map for psychotherapy. The beginning of the fairy tale portrays the origins of the self-alienation that lies behind the narcissistic wounding. At the start, the rejection by the attachment figure deeply damages the person's self-worth and almost casts a black cloud over them. As a result, the person ultimately rejects themselves and can no longer access their own feelings and needs, and this is symbolised in the banishment of the ravens to the glass mountain. The narcissistically wounded person is cut off from their own feelings and needs, as if they are behind glass. At the same time this defence, which protects the person from painful rejection of their needs, is highly fragile and can be broken, for example, by the occurrence of an illness. Because these people are so susceptible to injury, they often retreat into themselves, which the image of the banishment into the glass mountain can also stand for. The sister who sets out on the journey to find the lost brothers is an image of the Ego that is looking to reconnect to the lost feelings (of self-worth). The ring represents here a symbol for the function of relationships. What is meant by this is that the Ego does not give up the connection to the inner Self, to emotions, and to needs, but rather attempts to create or re-establish contact. This would initially be a helpful approach which the psychotherapy can take from the fairy tale. The fairy tale also makes it clear how tiring and prolonged this path is. The little stool which gets taken on the journey can be understood symbolically as an approach which allows the individual pace and time to investigate as well as also being a helpful therapeutic approach for narcissistically wounded people. The long journey also comes into being through the narcissistic person's attempt to stabilise themselves by keeping their wound, their suffering, away from their consciousness for as long as possible. The therapeutic approach is, therefore, precisely that of approaching the wound, the suffering, however painful it may be. The fairy tale lets the psychotherapist know that this approach can only happen slowly and the personality's protective measures designed to oppose the suffering are justified and must be acknowledged. On the path of approaching one's own woundedness, the Ego initially meets the unempathic, cold parental figures, and the experience of this must be remembered in the process of therapy. The sun and the moon represent these parents here, standing symbolically for the masculine, paternal and feminine, motherly figures. Because they are heavenly bodies, they also represent the narcissistically wounded person's pursuit of perfection; these people find it difficult to accept their own limitations and the limitations of relationships. The morning star, on the other hand, is equivalent in astronomy to the planet Venus, the goddess of love. This is portrayed by the fairy tale as a helpful key element, since the narcissistically wounded person needs love in order to restore his or her self-esteem, which in therapy is initially directed as a need to the person of the therapist. Here Asper recommends a specifically motherly rather than fatherly approach to therapy, therefore an approach which is shaped by understanding, sympathy, and empathy with the inner situation of the client. Because the affected person cannot find the necessary self-love within themselves, they must experience this loving approach for the first time in the therapeutic relationship.

The therapeutic experience shows, as can also be seen in the fairy tale, that after the reference to one's own childhood and the experience with one's own parents, the way inwards opens and the reference to one's own Self becomes possible. The key to this is self-love or self-appreciation. This is fragile, however, for narcissistic people and is lost over and over again, as is depicted in the fairy tale. Nevertheless, a certain inner stability is created, according to the fairy tale, which makes it possible for the Ego to find a solution in the crisis. Another archetypal element in the psychotherapeutic process comes to bear here, namely that a sacrifice must be made to find a solution. In the story, for example, the little finger must be cut off. For narcissistic people, it refers to giving up the claim of having complete control over oneself as well as over relationships with other people and learning to live with one's own limitations and the limitations of others. That makes possible, however, a great vitality and a better connection to one's own emotions and needs. The redemption of the ravens is an image for this inner split being overcome and the connection and reintegration of the rejected parts into the personality. Going home means coming back to oneself again and becoming oneself again – the recovery of the Ego-Self axis.

In this sense, myths and fairy tales are used as maps in Jungian psychotherapy for the formation of psychotherapeutic processes and its necessary stages. On a more comprehensive level, the individuation process outlined above provides a general map for psychotherapy, in which there is an almost archetypal development path: Persona – Shadow – Anima/ Animus – (Soul Image) – Old Sage/Great Mother – Self. This map helps the Jungian psychotherapist get their bearings and to orient themselves in the frequently chaotic material, made up by the patient's symptoms, complaints, stories, dreams, and other symbolic material. It must be noted, though, that these archetypal stages of the development process in psychotherapy do not simply progress in a linear fashion. Jung himself used the image of an upward spiral to describe how a patient might always return to the same points, but each time at a higher level. Clinical experience shows that it is not unusual to encounter symbolism of the Self's totality even at the start of a psychotherapeutic process, which then, however, disappears, so that the troubles of dealing with the shadow and with the soul image must be worked through to get back to it. The early contact with a feeling of wholeness and totality can act then as a promise that motivates the patients for the arduous work of psychotherapy. In other therapeutic schools something similar can be observed and described as the 'therapeutic honeymoon'.

This map of the individuation process as signposting what is worked through and differentiated as part of the psychotherapeutic process was essentially Jung's central interest in his life's work. He concerned himself, therefore, with mythology and religious stories and so on. With regards to the archetypal elements of this transformation process, he had particular success in the alchemy of the Middle Ages. A prominent example of this is Jung's interpretation of the late Middle Ages alchemical picture cycle of the Rosarium Philosophorum in his work *The Psychology of Transference* (Jung CW 16). Jung infers from this interpretation instructions for therapists on how they should focus on the client's transference in the therapeutic process.

5.2.3 *Case study of therapeutic work with archetypal dream elements*

Archetypes do not only, however, inform the psychotherapeutic process in an overarching way but also emerge in the form of defined symbols in dreams, images, or other symbolic material (Adam 2000). Here the principle also applies. The archetypal element transports more comprehensive information, for example, a more holistic perspective or a missing perspective on the problem at hand in the therapeutic process, which had not previously been available to consciousness. In psychotherapy, attempts are made, therefore, to make this comprehensive information, with the help of amplification and interpretation, accessible and useful for the therapeutic process. This is more fully explained in the following case study.

The patient registered for psychotherapy after he had served a prison sentence of some years for multiple cases of serious bodily harm. When he was released it had been recommended to him to go to psychotherapy. In prison the client had gone through a religious conversion and had become part of a fundamentalist Christian sect. He had gotten to grips completely with his violence, also with the help of the rigid morals of his sect, but he still suffered from intolerable states of tension, upheaval, and inner emptiness. The only thing that would help him combat these states was the consumption of pornographic videos, in particular those which contained violence against women. Then he could find inner peace, but would feel, however, burned out afterwards. After some time, his inner unrest built up again. The patient had grown up in extremely difficult family relationships and experienced a most traumatising childhood. His mother had a migratory background and his father had brought her from her homeland to Germany. His mother had even then never properly learned to speak German and was very awkward in social situations, according to the client. She may have had a mental disability. He was not able to respect his mother and had even later rejected her completely. He could not stand her body odour. Even as a child, she had always 'mollycoddled' him physically and 'groped' him, but 'did not understand what was going on'. The father was an alcoholic and had always beaten up one of the children when in a drunken state. Once the client was choked so badly around the throat by the father that he thought he would die. The mother had not been able to stop the father. When they were children, they would always have to try and recognise which state the father was in to potentially hide themselves from him. The father was unpredictable. When the patient was around 14 or 15 years old, he began to fight back and the father from then on left him in peace.

The father owned a huge collection of pornographic videos, which were hidden in a wall cabinet and which the client found extremely fascinating. Evidently, the father had a sexual obsession and spent so much money on prostitutes that he had almost brought the family to financial ruin on multiple occasions. The father had also been convicted of theft himself. In his youth, the client was taken in by a foster family because of his broken home situation and was apparently sexually abused by his foster mother. As soon as possible, the client then lived alone and became connected with a group of hooligans and skinheads, with whom he committed a variety of acts of violence which he was eventually convicted for.

Through these difficult conditions and the violence in the family, it can be assumed that the client had been heavily traumatised. This also explains the continually present depressive states. The former tendency towards violence can also be understood as a desperate attempt to compensate for the inner emptiness and the deep frustration of his needs. What is impressive is how he independently overcame these violent urges during his prison sentence and the orientation towards a strict moral structure that stabilised the weak Ego acting as a kind of rigid Superego. This can, however, not prevent the occurrence of states of deep inner emptiness. The consumption of violent pornographic videos can be understood as an addiction to combat the depression.

In the course of the six years of psychotherapy, numerous dreams were processed and worked through. The following list covers the entire period of the therapy.

1 I am walking down a street in the darkness. On the right and left are houses and fences. Groups of barking dogs jump against the fences. I'm afraid but then I become brave. I even bark aggressively at a dog and it becomes calm.

2 I am cycling uphill. It is strenuous. All around me are big trees. It's like in the mountains. Above is a small, white poodle which has barked and it is on a leash. I cycle on downhill as the road curves in tight corners. Dobermans are behind me but they aren't able to keep up with me because of the curves. They run next to me and bark at me. Then it's light and sunny. Above the pass it is beautiful. A restaurant, like in Italy, beautiful houses. Above on the pass black dogs are coming.

3 In standing water, a river? There's a jetty, someone is on the other side, they fall in the water. He is trapped under a piece of wood. I pull him out, but after hesitating. He is almost dead. But he has a box cutter and cuts the other helper's throat. I flee.

4 A picture: a cat that has been runover lies injured in the gutter and whimpers.

5 Dream from the youth: a car runs over the right paw of a cat (later I saw such a cat with a bandaged-up right paw in real life in front of our house)

6 (in black and white): At the station. A girl and another person, who seems masochistic, and a powerful black dog. The dog pulls the second person into the water with it, a pond, later it pulls them out of the water and up a slope. The person orally relieves themselves, then I see that he orally relieves the dog. Then at an apartment building. I say: the dog must be put on a leash. The masochistic person says: The dog has to be stroked. Me: No, he must be put on a leash and then go. The masochistic person is offended and goes into the apartment building. The other person says: you have to go after him, he's offended. The dog stunk. I rejected him and found him disgusting.

7 An old and bad smelling dog is with me and my girlfriend in Paris. He has run up to us. We got onto a bus, the dog wasn't able to come with us, we left him sitting outside. We

are already outside of the city, but we got back to the city on the motorway. The dog could not have run behind us.

8 I was the caretaker at a cafe in a house. I was kicked out (like Joseph in Potiphar's house). A father says goodbye to his little son, he is in the backyard. There is an old man with a pit bull. He says: I can show you how evil he is. I had to go straightaway though. I go up to a vineyard. The dog is loose and goes after me flashing his teeth, but I jump over fences and walls. The path goes up to the vineyard and down on the other side.

9 A small baby is in danger. I put on a diaper made of newspaper and take it with me through a system of pipes. Then, however, I forget it and leave it lying somewhere. Then I realise that it is missing and go back and find it again in the pipes. I pull it along some more and feed it. I thought: it is actually so small that it would need milk from a mother, but I gave it solid food.

10 I have a giant toe. The cuticle was really overgrown. I thought: that needs to be gotten rid of. It went back a little bit. There was another layer like the nail bed and it went down very easily. It didn't hurt at all, although I thought it would before. There were little black worms underneath, all rotten, but it could be wiped away very easily. Underneath, it was like new.

The most noticeable and consistently occurring element of these dreams is the symbol of the dog. This will now be amplified based on the representations in different symbol lexica:

In many cultures the dog is connected with death. In Egypt and Greece, a dog guards the kingdom of the dead (Cerberus, Anubis) and is a medium between the world of the living and the world of the dead. Nocturnal or ambiguous gods often appear in the form of a dog. The symbol of the dog has, therefore, a rather ambivalent meaning. It is associated on the one hand with wisdom, good, and piety (a white dog), but on the other hand also with emotions like impurity, vice, and envy (a dark dog). Dogs can also be considered to be connected with evil. In many cultures the dog appears as the forefather or creator of humanity and civilisation because of its alleged wisdom and sexual prowess. In different cultures, for example, in the Muslim world, dogs are considered to be unclean, because they are thought to be particularly sexually active and promiscuous (street dogs couple with each other without rules or boundaries). On the level of practical experience, the dog is a relationship animal; it is seen as a loyal friend of humans and has carried out many jobs for humans since the Neolithic period, for example, herding sheep, guarding the house, leading blind people, and so on.

This amplification of the dream symbol of the dog and its appearance in the various dreams against the background of the biographical case history makes it clear that a multiplicity of levels of meaning are condensed in a complex way in this kind of archetypal element. From the perspective of Jungian psychology, the dog embodies, at least in the first dreams of the series, a threatening complex that the patient has. On the one hand, this complex obviously reflects the experience with the violent father, and the experience of a real threat from the father's unpredictable violence is reflected in the threat of the dogs. On the other hand, the violence the patient describes can also be represented by the dogs' aggression. At the beginning of the therapy this violence was not yet really controlled by the Ego and therefore threatened and called into question the ability of the Ego to truly control and direct. Interestingly, the multifaceted significance of an obsessive sexuality in the life of the patient can also be found, however, in the symbol of the dog, whether this is the fascination with the father's obsession or the patient's own sexual behaviour. The dog as gatekeeper to the underworld is here an evident symbol for the patient's ambivalent and unsolved relationship with his own 'underground' impulses of compulsive sexuality and violence.

The dog as an archetypal symbol, however, does not only depict a mental reality, but also contains, as with all archetypes, an inner dynamic which relates to the polarity inherent to it. As was clear in the amplification, the dog has positive as well as negative connotations. In the dream series it is clear to see that in the course of the therapy – and supposedly also dependent on the therapeutic process – the meaning of the symbol changes and a change in the relationship between the Ego and the complex takes place. After a while, the positive aspects of the symbol appear more frequently, here particularly the relationship function. In the symbol of the injured animal or the animal requiring help, the Ego is prompted to caringly address these needy parts of its own personality. This is initially difficult for the Ego as disgust and rejection towards these parts of the personality dominate. As the therapy progresses, however, the Ego finally manages to behave in a more or less caring and applied way towards this part, at which point they change from the form of an animal to the form of a human infant, which can be understood when regarded psychodynamically as a development towards a greater awareness and integration. This corresponds with the results of the therapy, since at the end of it the patient had now married, started a family, completed a solid professional training, and acquired a good position in a highly sophisticated job. In every respect, he was socially and professionally well integrated. From time to time depressive moods did indeed occur, but the patient had increasingly successfully been able to turn to his partner for his needs and relied less on violent pornography to overcome these situations.

The dream series presented here also makes it clear that different levels of meaning are interwoven and depicted in complex ways in an archetypal symbol. The archetype has, therefore, a representative function for the inner mental situation, and at the same time there is a significant dynamic embedded in the archetype. In this dynamic the polarity inherent within the archetype has the ability to balance out or expand and complete the previous imbalance (here: violence, denial of one's own needs, disconnected compulsive sexuality) with its antithesis (here: increasing relatedness, acceptance of one's own needs, communication instead of violence). The Jungian psychotherapy is designed to set in motion and support this process of balancing out and achieving entirety of the personality through working with archetypal symbols. Of course, the different levels of making the unconscious level of meaning of archetypes conscious, the experience of the therapeutic relationship, and other therapeutic interventions as well as the lived daily experience of the patient flow into one another in complex ways. It is also not always the case that in the course of a psychotherapy a certain archetypal symbol, as is the case here, stands in the foreground. In other cases, a variety of archetypal elements play a role, or there is a chain of archetypal symbols connected with each other. An excellent example for the latter is the dream series presented by Jung in his publication *Dream Symbols of the Individuation Process* (CW, 12).

5.2.4 Archetypal transference

Along with the application of the archetype concept in psychotherapy presented here, for Jung there is the specific term 'archetypal transference'. What is meant by this is that an archetypal element, which describes a basic mental quality or an aspect of personality, is not initially experienced as something which belongs to the affected person but is rather projected onto another. In the context of therapy, it would be projected onto the psychotherapist and it then shapes how this other is perceived. The classic example of this mechanism which Jung describes, comes from the famous film *Matter of Heart*, in which Jung was asked extensively about his psychology and his life by an English journalist. Jung discusses here the case of a patient, a young woman, who developed a hugely idealised transference towards him. Jung frequently appeared in the dreams that she processed in the course of the therapy and consistently in the form of an informed authority, father figure, luminary, and so on. This was epitomised in a dream in which the patient experienced lying in Jung's arms. Jung himself was a giant figure and stood in a cornfield, over which the wind was blowing, and the giant figure of Jung with the patient in his arms swayed to the rhythm of the wind back and forth, like a father who rocks his baby to sleep.

Jung inferred that because the cornfield in the dream is mature and ready to harvest, the patient herself is mature and ready to process the solution of this transference. He amplified first for her the dream image with material from religious stories in which, for example, god appears as the wind and indicated to her finally the transference as an image of an inner god, that she cannot, however, consider as belonging to herself because of her deep self-esteem disorder. If she could accept that these qualities of being taken up into god's arms, of inner authority and so on, actually belong to herself, this would be the way to overcome her deep self-doubt.

This case study makes the fundamental mechanism of archetypal transference clear. An as yet unlived, unseparated part of one's own personality, a mental quality, emerges from the unconscious in the form of an archetypal image, which is initially, however, not experienced as something belonging to oneself but rather only perceivable in the projection onto another. In this sense the projection as Jung understands it is also not only a defence mechanism, but rather a meaningful and development-oriented mental process in which an as yet unconscious part of oneself is experienceable for the first time. Typically, in this archetypal transference the proximity to the idealised other is looked for, which makes possible a concrete experience with the respective quality. As part of this process, the other is, however, perceived in a very heavily distorted fashion and not recognised as they are in reality. What is then finally needed is that which Jung calls the 'retraction of the projection/transference'. It is necessary for the person to recognise the projection as such and realise that what they perceive as the other does not really belong to the other, but rather to the person themselves. Only then can it be integrated into the personality as one's own, lived quality/ability.

This concept was later extended by Peter Schellenbaum (1995) to the so-called *Leitbildspiegelung* (guiding image). It represents a fundamental mental mechanism in which one's as yet unlived qualities/abilities/competences are initially brought out in the form of projections, and finally in a thoroughly arduous process are slowly made conscious and integrated. This is particularly interesting as Jungian psychology can also be considered as a psychology thoroughly oriented around the individual. Here, however, a deeply interpersonal, interactive process of becoming conscious of archetypal contents is described, one which requires a relationship and indeed can only actually take place in a current lived relationship. This mechanism will be discussed further in the context of archetype theory being used in couple therapy.

5.2.5 The archetype of the wounded healer as an orientation for a psychotherapeutic approach

The relationship between the healer and the sick person, between the psychotherapist and the patient, also revolves around an archetypal constellation. If someone looks to a healer for the solution to their suffering, then, at least according to Jung's psychology, the archetypal healer-patient constellation is activated. This archetype is by nature configured in a polarised way – healer and patient form aspects which are related to one another. Each person who is an actor in such a constellation carries in principle both parts in them, that of the healer as well as the wounded person (Hofmann & Roesler 2010, Frick 1996). Jung's assertion that 'only where the doctor himself is affected, can he have an effect [...] Only the wounded heal' (Jaffe 1971, p. 139) became famous in this context. Jung used the ancient myth of Chiron, the wounded healer from Greek mythology, to describe this archetypal constellation and its dynamic (see Merchant 2012). Chiron, the centaur, was a hybrid creature, in which godly, human, and animal attributes were united. He was formed of the hindquarters and legs of a horse and the head, body, and arms of a human. Chiron emerged from the union of the Greek titan Kronos and the nymph Thalia. Since Thalia was ashamed of her centaur son's form and Kronos also left him, Chiron grew up without his loving parents (a first wound to the psyche). He was raised by his foster father, Apollo, the god of music, divination, and healing and was instructed by him in these arts. During a feast, at which wine was flowing freely, Chiron was accidently hit by one of Heracles' arrows. Because the tip of this arrow was soaked in the blood of the Hydra, the half-god Chiron, who as the son of a titan and a nymph possessed the privilege of immortality and was considered the greatest healer of his time, was not himself in a position to heal his own wound. He was, indeed, capable of healing the wounds of others, but with regards to his own wound it was unfortunately not possible. In Jung's interpretation, the ability to heal others is connected irresolvably with one's own wounding and the inability to heal oneself.

> It is not too much of an exaggeration to say that about half of every far-reaching treatment consists of self-examination by the doctor and then only when he puts something right in himself can he also help the patient. It is not wrong when he is struck and affected by the patient. He is only in a position to heal in accordance with his own wounding. The Greek myth of the wounded doctor says nothing more than that.
>
> (Jung CW 16, §239)

Thus, Jung saw it as almost a prerequisite that the doctor, therapist, or healer had their own wounds and had made themselves aware of them because only this gave them the ability to establish a therapeutic relationship with the patient which contributed to the healing. This was also the reason why Jung, even at the beginning of the psychoanalytical movement, vehemently supported the inclusion of a mandatory training analysis in the training of prospective psychotherapists.

In traditional medicine systems, for example, shamanism or the cult of Asklepios, the vocation, authority, and the effectiveness of healers were often considered as being connected to their own experience of being wounded and were legitimised in this way. The wounds were not understood as a sign of fragility or failure, but rather as an indication that a test had been passed and as a sign of acquired wisdom. Thus, the future shaman had lived the chaos of a temporary, profound dissolution of the inner and outer order on their own body. The shaman, as a pre-image of the wounded healer, was required to subject themselves to the action of uncontrollable archetypal energies and forces in order to finally acquire a greater totality and access to the previously inaccessible dimension of reality and healing. A variety of images of the descent to the underworld and the return from it can also be found in Greek mythology, which can be understood as the individuation path to a more comprehensive integrity of the soul.

The image of the wounded healer thus resonates with the fact that he has made his way into the underworld of mental and physical suffering in his own experience and has emerged from it changed for the better. This points to, of course, Jung's own confrontation with his unconscious in 1913/14, as he has documented in the so-called 'Red Book'.

From the point of view of analytical psychology, therefore, the good analyst is also a healer who is themselves wounded, who has experienced and reflected on his woundedness in the 'night sea voyage' within the framework of his own training analysis, which makes it possible for him embark on this journey into the unconscious with his patient, accompany them, and be a guide on this path. Moreover, this means that a 'liminal' space forms between the therapist and the patient as part of the analysis, which is not wholly of this world so to speak, which is open to the archetypal influences of the unconscious, and in which a healing relationship experience can be constructed. It is important to emphasise with this, that this event is not subject to the wilful direction and control of the analyst. Jung always emphasised that the psychotherapy can be only successful 'Deo concedente – God willing'. This concerns the recognition of the fundamental limits of any therapeutic action. This can also be seen in the myth of Chiron. As a half-god and as the greatest healer of all, Chiron was not able to heal himself. The recognition of one's own limits protects from hubris and opens for the healer the gateway to a deeper compassion and healing.

As we have seen, the wound is the entrance to the inner world and to the possibility of a transmission between the 'lower' and 'upper' worlds, or between the unconscious and consciousness. The figure of Chiron also stands for this in a symbolic way. The centaur, a hybrid between a horse and a human, is an image for the ability of the therapist, who has ideally created or can ideally create a good connection between his consciousness and his unconscious.

In Jung's work, however, the significance of the therapist's wounding goes beyond the ability to mediate between the worlds. In his concepts of the transference relationship or of the therapeutic relationship in general, Jung indicates that a psychotherapy is particularly effective when a direct relationship forms between the unconsciouses of both therapist and patient, almost a third area in which both people are at least temporarily coalescent and strongly and mutually influence one another. What is special about this area is that it is no longer only related to the personalities of both participants, but rather is open to the collective unconscious and its archetypal structural elements and is intensely influenced by these. This space can develop its healing effect, however, precisely because of this. Jung used the so-called marriage quaternio to explain the diverse transference and countertransference relationships between the therapist and the patient in his work *The Psychology of the Transference* (CW 16). In this work he focuses on the direct relationship between the unconscious of the therapist and that of the patient, what he calls in his work the 'participation mystique'.

In recent years, this concept of the direct unconscious relationship between therapist and client has been expanded in analytical psychology to the concept of an interactive field (Stein 1995, Schwartz-Salant 1995, 1998). What is meant by this is that, through the intense emotional relationship as part of the analytical psychotherapy, a shared unconscious space is created between the therapist and the client, which is more than just the two unconsciouses of each partner. This shared unconscious space can be regarded as something of a third space, that possesses almost its own mental life and own regularities. 'Analytical psychology can most likely have a great effect in this area, in which both sides are mutually, unconsciously influenced [...] it is the sphere where different elements of both analytical partners coalesce' (Jacoby 1993, p. 57).

> In this conception of the field, the personal factors, gained in one's own past, are combined with an objective substratum, Jung's collective unconscious. This space can be seen to have its own dynamic, which is separated and independent from the individual. Nevertheless, this dynamic can only be experienced through the individual and shared subjectivities

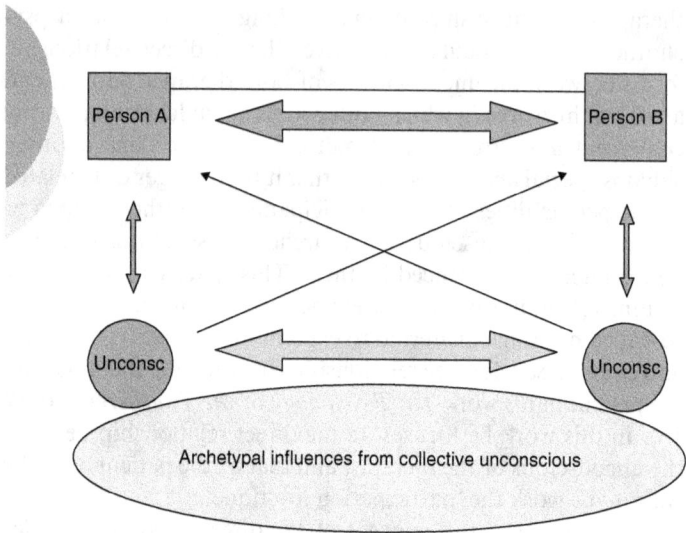

Figure 5.1 Marriage quaternio – the conscious and unconscious relationship between therapist and client as well as uncon-
scious/archetypal factors which influence it.

of both participants. The experience of becoming conscious
of this is in itself deeply healing. This understanding of the
space, that encompasses both dimensions, the subjective
and the objective, can be described as an interactive field.
That interactive field is between the collective unconscious
and the sphere of subjectivity and likewise it encompasses
both.

(Schwartz-Salant 1995, p. 2)

The psychoanalytical terms of the transitional space
(Winnicott) and the analytical third (Ogden) have similar
meanings.

The concept of the interactive field assumes, then, that a
psychotherapy (or indeed every healer-patient relationship)
has a greater healing effect if this third area between the two

participants forms. This also makes it possible for archetypal healing factors, which in modern terms would be described as self-healing powers of the psyche and the organism, to have an effect. This has, however, certain prerequisites on the side of the healer, and these are made possible first and foremost through being conscious of their own wounding. This is a therapeutic attitude, whose intention is not primarily to get rid of the symptoms, not absolutely to strive for something certain in the sense of a plan, of what the goal would be, or what would be good for the patient. It is rather a matter of getting involved in the constellation that arises, of allowing what happens, and also of allowing oneself to be drawn into it so that one is also wounded (with some clients this is not possible in any other way than to simply suffer at first) and to remain aware of what is happening. 'The right attitude is one which allows the unconscious to co-operate rather than opposing it' (Jung, CW 16, p. 366). Jung emphasises that the healer also encounters a part of their own wholeness in each patient, therefore the patient's wounding is also always a piece of their own. This relates to the mysterious process of client and therapist 'being found', thus the coming into being of this unique therapeutic relationship is directed by a comprehensive whole, in which the wounding of the healer plays an essential role. Accordingly, Jung also emphasised that both parties always emerge out of a good therapy changed by the process, the patient as well as the therapist.

5.2.6 Using the archetype concept to explain the dynamic in couple relationships and its use in couple therapy

From what has been presented here, it will be clear that the dynamic of the individuation process can develop primarily in intense interpersonal relationships, like for example, the analytical relationship, where in complex ways both individuals and their unconsciouses are intertwined with each other. When Jung coined the term 'individuation', he emphasised that this cannot take place in one's own space, but rather it needs the relationship and the conflict with other humans. The individuation process 'is not only a subjective process of integration, but rather also an essential objective relationship process' (Jung CW 16, p. 448). 'Without consciously acknowledged and accepted relatedness to other people there is no synthesis of the personality whatsoever' (ibid., p. 444). It would be a misunderstanding to see individuation as a process which isolated the person. Times of withdrawal and transformation from inside may be a necessary part of the individuation process, but they are not, however, the ultimate aim. The inner centring acquired in the individuation process must finally also prove its worth, especially in dealing with other people and the associated conflicts that come with this. In his concern with alchemy, Jung was even clearer about this point:

> Alchemy considers the psyche to be a half-mental, half-physical substance, a hermaphroditic essence that unites opposites and never manifests itself in people without a relationship to another. The man without relationships has no wholeness, because he can only achieve them through the soul, which on the other hand cannot exist without the other side, which is always found in the 'you'. Totality or wholeness are created from the connection of the 'I' with the 'You'.
>
> (Ibid., p. 451)

Alongside the analytical relationship, these ideas can also be used to explain the mental dynamic in romantic relationships. A central idea in the archetype concept is that mental life is based on opposing tensions and the compensation of imbalance. Jung assumed that for every mental quality there is a shadow or an opposite power in their archetypal root, and mental energy comes from their tension. As part of its constructive direction, oriented around integrity, the unconscious is prepared to equalise or to compensate the possible imbalances in the conscious personality. For this, it uses the tension of the opposite pairs. The archetypes, the great psychological issues are organised as polarities which are connected with each other. That is, one-sidedness in a system is compensated by its opposite, and this opposite may not be present in that person, but rather in others with whom the person has a close emotional relationship, for example, children or even partners (for parallel conceptions in psychoanalysis, see Dicks 1967). The Self gives the individuation the direction in that it contains within it a certain amount of unconscious knowledge about the potential integrity of the personality, which also includes the shadow sides of the person. It can be argued here that a romantic relationship offers a field unlike any other sphere in life, in which individuation is initiated and promoted because here, as in no other relationship, we are connected with our entire inner being to our partner and at the same time exposed; therefore, we are also confronted with our own dark sides and those of our partner and cannot avoid them. Jung commented that:

> Such a conflict as this is not at all possible without a relationship to another human. A general, academic insight into one's errors is ineffective, because the errors do not really occur, but rather only their impression. But they become acute when they really come to the fore in the relationship with a fellow human being and become noticeable to both oneself and the other. Only there can they really be felt and recognized in their true nature.
>
> (Jung CW 16, p. 221)

We can assume that the unconscious plays a part in the choice of a life partner, that it even has the largest part in the choosing of a partner. The unconscious allows us to choose a partner who initiates conflicts with us precisely on those points around which we have an unresolved essential mental issue, or where we are supposed to realise a development potential in ourselves. In principle, our Ego does not choose the partner, but rather the Self with its view of the totality of the personality. The Self allows us to choose a partner who calls for individuation and who drives us towards the potential inside of us, the wholeness of our personality. That means the conflicts which we experience with our partner are actually an appeal to us, telling us that we must struggle with these points ourselves and we must develop ourselves further (Roesler 2011). Totality in Jung's sense means not the ability to function but rather a realisation of all the possibilities and abilities which are embedded in us, as well as a reconciliation with everything that we are, including the parts of us which we still reject. The path to wholeness, therefore, is also often painful and, most importantly, it cannot be obtained without conflicts. In approaching our possible integrity, however, we find the meaning in our life. We experience then that we are really the person that we can be and that we live the life that was meant for us, that we realise our inherent potential. Thus, the psyche searches for a certain partner because it unconsciously feels that this person will help come into contact with the rejected and unlived parts of one's own personality. It could be said that this is the reason why all people search for a couple relationship with such energy. Essentially, we are all searching for wholeness and integrity.

Couple therapy normally begins with the following situation (Roesler 2011). Both partners argue and accuse one another of having certain difficult aspects to their character, deficits in certain areas and so on. If these accusations are more precisely examined, it then becomes apparent that the problems which both see in the other revolve around a shared inner issue. Both partners stand in opposition with regards to this shared theme, almost as extreme polar opposites. What we have here is, in Jungian terms, a constellation of opposites and a shared archetypal theme. These opposing tensions lead to a polarisation in romantic relationships as the relationship develops. These polarisations revolve around existential, psychological themes, for example, antithetical pairings, which determine mental life for all people and must be balanced out in long-term romantic relationships. The following list gives an idea of these themes, but is in no way exhaustive:

- Closeness – Distance
- Commitment – Isolation
- Attachment – Autonomy
- Dependence – Independence
- Weakness – Strength
- Submission – Dominance

- Grandiosity – Inferiority (self-worth)
- Community – Self-will
- Introversion – Extroversion
- Activity – Passivity
- Change – Resistance
- Irrational – Rational
- Feeling – Reason
- Release – Control
- Acceptance – Confrontation
- Cooperation – Competition
- Merger – Separation

It seems that two partners, who both have a complex, meaning a problem grounded in their previous experiences, in the same thematic area, find themselves in a relationship (in part an unconscious choice), and then in the course of this relationship a polarisation arises, so that each partner moves to the opposing poles of each theme. That means that in the unconscious choice of a partner, each person searches for a partner who is almost the opposite to their own unconscious and unresolved problems. At the beginning of the relationship, that is frequently precisely what is fascinating and attractive about the partner, and if both partners are asked what they found attractive about each other at the start, they often cite those things which now disturb or irritate them. When this is looked at more closely, there is often a vague, largely unconscious fantasy that one's own problems can be solved in connection with this person, or at least they will no longer be felt to be obstructive. Regarded from the perspective of the Self, the significance of this connection is that one's own issues can be best processed and worked through with this partner because in the relationship they must inevitably be confronted. The polarisation described above is a process, which initially takes place in a romantic relationship and can frequently last many years. Both partners already bring a certain bias with them from their past, which is only allocated a role during the course of the partner relationship. First of all, this serves as a defence against projecting one's own unsolved and unlived issues onto others. As we have seen above, however, this process of projection, in the sense of the 'guiding image', can be understood as a meaningful process for individuation. On closer examination, it appears that precisely those qualities of the partner that have now been rejected, which have perhaps been distorted into extremes, are missing or poorly developed in one's own life. The initially undeveloped worth, lying in the unconscious as potential worth, is projected onto the other and can only be perceived there, either as something fascinatingly foreign or unknown, or as something not worth to be combatted. This projection, however, is the path to be able to bring out the as yet undeveloped value from ourselves and to face up to it. We can initially only perceive this quality in another, in the projection. The next step is, then, to recognise that this is a projection, that what I actually see in others is actually something from inside myself. The last step is to take this projection back onto myself, thus, to develop this characteristic or capability in myself, in my own life, so that it becomes a part of my personality. Jung remarks in relation to this that (CW 16) '[the process] wants us to surrender to a You, which seems to consist of all those qualities that we have not realised as our own'. In a romantic relationship, the person projects something onto the partner which they can become themselves, an archetypal potential which they can become conscious of and realise in their own life. Both partners have something real about them that makes the projection possible, whereby they simultaneously have a common unconscious theme that contains an archetypal core. Both bring an imbalance with them which compliments the imbalance of the other. In this way, the described polarisation arises as the relationship progresses, which can be understood, in the sense of the interactive field described above, as a complex unconscious interactive relationship. This in turn leads to a relationship dynamic that can become fruitful because it forces them both to deal with the shared unconscious theme.

The model of couple dynamics suggested here assumes that, just as in an analytical relationship, an interactive field forms in a romantic relationship in which the transformation processes and dynamics associated with this concept take place. Just as Jung had described how an archetype takes hold of individuals and they act them out, this can also be said of couples, that they integrate themselves in archetypical scenarios and these will be enacted again and again. Anyone who has experience in a long-term romantic relationship knows the experience of getting into regularly recurring, stereotypical patterns of conflict, and just as regularly asking oneself afterwards why something so trivial had been so irritating and why over the years you haven't gotten over it. Evidently, these destructive patterns of interaction have a larger power over the partners than their conscious wills, but this is precisely what is characteristic of archetypal influences. Different Jungian authors have extensively described these couple archetypes (e.g., Haule 2004, Kast 1984).

If the partners can understand these processes as spheres of both growth and the individual, then something communal can grow with time, something that represents a new entity. This entity would be the relationship as a 'united binary', where both are not only separate but also melded together, and not in a negative sense, the ultimate goal of Opus.

1   'The mental marriage with one's own soul image as an inner experience' (that would be the individual integrity aspect)
2   Being able to recognise the reality of the other person, thus liberated from the projections and being able to have a real relationship with that person.

   And just as there is still an essential split in the alchemical end product, so will the painful feeling of the dual-nature never truly be lost. The aim is only important as an idea, essential, however, is the opus that leads to the goal.

                                                        (Jung CW 16)

A case study: 'No space for the other'

The couple came to couple therapy on the advice of the clinic where the woman had been treated because of severe depression. This was preceded by years of an overly altruistic defence of her basic depressive disorder. She describes in her own words how she 'was always only there for others', until she fell into a serious depressive condition of exhaustion. Her husband had suffered for years from an anxiety disorder, but this was being successfully treated in psychotherapy. As long as he depended on her strength, she worked smoothly for him and the two children. When he, however, emerged from his disorder and threw himself with a whole new life energy into the expansion of the bakery and pastry shop he ran, she broke down and had to be hospitalised. A polarisation of strength against weakness existed here, of a caregiver and a dependent or someone who must be given constant consideration. After the woman had played the role of caregiver for years, this relationship was turned upside down as his problems improved. She became the person in need and now claimed the same consideration for herself. In this way, the polarisation had developed further in the direction of the fundamental problem, namely egoism versus altruism. After she had fulfilled the altruistic role for years, the wife had now been put into the position of the person in need. This relatively sudden shift into the opposite position is described by Jung as 'enantiodromia'. This can frequently be seen in strongly polarised couples, for example, when a partner changes their position as a result of individual therapy, maybe becoming more autonomous, and the other suddenly takes on the previously avoided opposite position as a result.

Her position as the person in need could be clearly seen in her sandplay picture. Only the left side of the tray, the side of the unconscious, was used, which indicates a strongly regressive condition. She is surrounded here by all the people 'who want something from me'. It was, however, interesting that in the bottom left corner, thus in the area closest to the unconscious, something green and new was growing, that the client was protecting behind a wall and a fence. She herself said that if she could withdraw there, she would be fine. Due to her unconscious pattern, however, she could rarely afford to do so.

In his sandplay picture, the husband portrayed his development from the anxiety and weakness to a new strength and energy, a very progressive line of development, running from left to right, which culminated in a tiger and a strong muscle man. What is interesting is that an image representing his wife was initially missing. When asked to put this one figure in the picture, he placed it on the edge of the sandbox where it literally 'fell down the back' again and again; it could not be expressed more clearly that there was no room in his life for his wife at the moment, which of course she felt very strongly. With this, the theme and the aim of the therapy was again brought into focus. For him the recurring question was: 'How can you make space in your life for your wife and for her needs?' (thus moving from the fully egoist position in the direction of altruism and to integrating this position). For her, the invitation to take as much space as possible for retreating to her 'good place' was also a symbol for learning self-care and taking herself seriously (that is, learning and integrating egoism).

5.2.7 The use of the archetype concept in therapeutic encounter groups: an example from the men's movement

As has already been mentioned above, a whole series of publications on men's movements and the psychology of men have appeared, in particular in archetypal psychology (Bly 1990, Moore & Gillette 1991), and these draw on the archetype concept. Now, on the basis of these publications, elaborate concepts on how to design self-awareness oriented men's groups exist. As an example of such an application and its reference to the archetype concept, we can consider the concept of a self-awareness group for men (Schick 2015). The group, which is designed for around 15 men and to run from between one and a half to two years, also uses elements from initiatic therapy alongside the archetype concept, as well as systemic approaches. The progression of the group is oriented around the previously mentioned hero's journey. Hero is also understood here as a symbol for the Ego, which brings out the courage to face one's inner being and the shadow sides, and to find more authenticity and wholeness on the way to oneself. The seminar goes through a series of seven archetypes which can be regarded as characteristic of masculine identity and the different sides of a man: healer, father, warrior, wild man, lover, mystic, and king. Here is a description of the archetype of the father as an example:

The large field of tension of the father archetype is that between support/empowerment on the one hand and challenge/threat on the other hand. If both of these poles are in a healthy balance, the son can develop his aggressive parts and his commitment. The essence of this archetype is supportive strength. The archetype of the father is explicitly conceptualized as polarized. There is a supportive, healthy, empowering, aggressive, retentive side and a challenging, injuring, destructive side. When approaching the father archetype, it is a matter of taking the father as a whole – with both sides – and experiencing him as a supportive and encouraging power.

(Schick 2015, p. 44)

As effective for the development of the personality as these seminar concepts might be, it must be said that this application of the archetype concept does not fit with Jung's sense of it. In the classic approach of analytical psychology, certain archetypes would not be presented to the client, but would rather be used only as a background canvas to explain the phenomena which are present in the client. Thus, the archetypes provide the therapist with a map which is, however, often not explicitly labelled at all.

5.3 Applications in cultural studies

Parallel to the clinical use of the archetype concept, it was used from the beginning as an explanation for intercultural convergences in fairy tales, myths, religious ideas, and the traditions of tribes, and also by Jung himself. The basic idea of this application of the archetype concept in cultural studies is that the formation of collective ideas, religious forms, and social processes is influenced by the archetypes underlying mental life. In turn, from knowledge of the underlying archetypes, the dynamic and the inherent meaning of these collective forms can be inferred. The archetypes also act here as a map, with which the underlying, general human universals in the variety of social and cultural manifestations become visible. Moreover, this map allows the inherent logic of the fundamental, archetypal structure in apparently irrational dynamics and modern social and political processes to be recognised.

5.3.1 Cultural psychology: analysis of mythological narratives

As was mentioned above, since the nineteenth century, a high degree of concurrence had been noted in the myths and folk tales of different peoples. One of the most prevalent narratives is the myth of the hero's journey, which can be reduced to a few general structural elements. The hero takes on a situation problematic for his community (e.g., a dragon threatening the land), takes the fight to this overpowering opponent completely alone, and finally overcomes him, although it is not believed possible at first. He receives help, however, from fantastical figures (e.g., speaking animals) to do this. Often, he also liberates an imprisoned maiden whom he later marries (Propp 1975). Analytical psychology can explain the similarities of the myths and fairy tales as well as the universal prevalence of the narrative. Because an archetypal structure underlies the narrative, we find it everywhere in the world throughout time, and therefore all people are fascinated by this story. With this in mind, a concern with myths and fairy tales has a long tradition in the world of analytical psychology. Fairy tales and myths are here interpreted as deeply psychological because one hopes to gain insights into the archetypal basic structures presented in them. With this it is important to note that the archetypes in fairy tales and myths exist in narrative form. As a science of narration and narrative forms, narratology as a special field of linguistics has long been concerned with the investigation of narratives, completely independently of analytical psychology. It can be maintained that narratives adhere fundamentally to a congruent basic structure. So if a narrative is worth being told, there must be a break with expectation, which can be generally grasped as the starting problem. The fairy tale then describes, through peaks and troughs, sometimes in the form of an elevation to a climax and a turning point, the path to the solution of the problem.

Thus, in this way the narrative essentially describes the path to a problem's solution. If this is considered in conjunction with the perspective of Jungian psychology, that certain narratives, like myths and fairy tales, depict archetypal basic structures, it can be said that archetypal routes from an initial problem to a solution can be found in narrative form. Since these archetypal structures, moreover, describe problematic situations that are common for all humans and the way to solve them, it becomes clear why these are also so interesting for a clinically oriented analytical psychology. Insofar as the general structures for the solution or transformation of universal human problems can be found in fairy tales and myths, a psychological interpretation of these narrative forms is very helpful in order to find, using the narratives, structures for psychotherapeutic applications. In the concrete clinical work with fairy tales and myths, the analytical psychotherapist attempts to create structural coherence between the client's life situation or his fantasies or dreams, and the fairy tales or myths, because this provides indications of the archetypal structures underlying the client's problem as well as archetypal structures that can contribute to a therapeutic change in the situation. The notion of Jung and those who came after him was that every fairy tale and every myth depicted a stage of the individuation process in narrative form. In this way, the concern within analytical psychology with fairy tales and myths aims to be able to better understand and depict the individuation process as a map of the psyche and its development process. In particular, the Jung scholar Marie Louise von Franz (1986, 1991, 1997) has been concerned intensely over many years with the interpretations of fairy tales from all over the world and has published widely on this topic. The conclusion of her interpretation of fairy tales is summarised in the work of one of her colleagues, Hedwig von Beit (1952–1957), and organised based on the central archetypal narratives which can be found across the world. More recently, the Jungian Verena Kast has dealt with the interpretation of fairy tales and their application in psychotherapy in numerous publications. Depth psychological interpretations of biblical stories can be found in Drewermann (2003).

In order to illustrate the depth psychology approach to fairy tales and myths, a myth and its depth psychology interpretation will be outlined in detail. Homer's *Odyssey* has been selected because, first, almost no other myth gives such a comprehensive representation of the stages of the individuation process and, secondly, the *Odyssey* certainly depicts one of the most central myths of Western culture. Drewermann (1984) and von Franz (1986) have written at length on approaches to the interpretation of fairy tales. Fundamentally, the interpretation of a fairy tale or myth can be considered on the subjective level. This is originally an interpretation perspective that was developed for the interpretation of dreams in psychotherapy. What is meant by this is that all figures and objects that appear in dreams or myths, or indeed essentially the whole landscape of the narrative, are considered as a part of the dream's inner world or, in the case of the myth, the human psyche in general. For this, it is important to realise how myths and fairy tales are formed. In analytical psychology, it was suspected early on that the fairy tales of societies originally developed out of individuals' dreams. Even today, in traditional tribes the very widely prevalent custom can be found that the members of a group tell each other in the morning the dreams of the previous night. If a dream contains a particularly large number of archetypal elements (in Jungian psychology this is described as a 'great dream'), then it can be assumed that this dream speaks to many members of the group because it touches on their archetypal structures. Consequently, this dream is told and spread to the group and in the process of this proliferation individual elements of the dream increasingly fall away, so that after many generations the story is reduced to its fundamental archetypal structure. This would then be the fairy tale. For myths, it is rather to be assumed that real events, or at least elements of them, rather than dreams, are underlying. Thus, it is known that Homer's *Iliad* is based on a real war around the city of Troy, which has been excavated in present-day Turkey and in whose walls traces of fire from the corresponding time period have been found. We can, therefore, imagine that a myth begins at least initially as a legend about real actions and experiences of prominent personalities (the heroes of the myths), which are proliferated within a culture, for example, from wandering bards. In the process of this proliferation, the real stories are then passed on with increasingly fantastical elements, which are inspired by archetypal structures (e.g., speaking animals, monsters and creatures, heavenly figures, and so on). After many generations of the passing on of this story, it no longer chiefly concerns the report of the real events but rather the telling itself, which speaks to the psyche of the people because it represents archetypal structures. Here, particularly the figure of the hero proper and his hero's journey should be mentioned. From the perspective of depth psychology, the hero can be understood as a personification of an Ego consciousness that in light of a problematic psychological situation, for example, the demand for a transformation and renewal of the personality, takes the task of descending into its own inner depth to search for a new orientation of life and meaning from the archetypal structures found there and to renew oneself on this basis. The motive of the night journey can be found, therefore, in almost all hero myths (and also in many fairy tales). The hero must take themselves into the depths, the underworld, the lair of the dragon, or in any case a situation of extreme danger and exposure, in order to find the treasure they seek (an imprisoned maiden, the water of life, and so on) and to bring it back to the surface. This would be a very general archetypal image for the process that, according to Jung's understanding, is also sought in psychotherapy. It revolves around a letting in of one's own unconscious in order to correct or inspire consciousness through the contents of one's own unconscious. This process can then lead to a transformation and a new orientation of the personality, ultimately an expansion and extension in the direction of one's own integrity. The protagonist is, therefore, a hero, because he takes on this adventure and the connected fears that come with it, and endures them to experience a solution to the problem and a renewal. The dragons and monsters of fairy tales and myths are ultimately, regarded from a depth psychology perspective, our own fears and unresolved complexes. Interestingly, in fairy tales and myths the hero is regularly supported by helpful figures in his journey into the darkness. This is of course particularly interesting for the psychotherapeutic process, if this aspect can be understood and translated into a psychological language. This is precisely what the depth psychology interpretation of fairy tales and myths attempts to do. What follows is an exemplification of the *Odyssey* in this way.

The Odyssey – *a journey through the unconscious and a process of self-development*

Homer's *Odyssey*, along with the *Iliad*, can be considered one of the central Western myths. They were both written down around 800 BCE but existed well before this in oral form. They essentially describe the return journey of the king of Ithaca, Odysseus, from his participation in the Trojan War back to his home island and his wife, Penelope. This hero's journey is a quest, as is typical for many heroes (Percival searches for the grail, Siegfried searches for the treasure of the Nibelungen, Gilgamesh for immortality, and so on). These searches on the return journey can be understood from a depth psychology perspective as the search for the inner homeland, in Jungian terms for the Self, the centre of one's personality. Odysseus can be understood in this case as a personification of a strengthened Ego consciousness who, unlike his comrades, can concentrate on the imaginary centre of the journey, namely the Self. That Odysseus is a consciousness hero, thus a bringer of consciousness, can be also be seen in his epithet 'the cunning', and his conscious abilities, his intellectual acumen, his foresight, and his ability to plan are emphasised not only in the *Odyssey* but also in the *Iliad*. In the *Iliad* it is Odysseus' plan to build the Trojan horse to smuggle soldiers into the besieged city of Troy and ultimately to win the war for the Greeks. After the war is won, Odysseus sets out with his companions and ten ships on the journey to his home island, Ithaca. In the course of the journey he loses all his companions to enemy tribes, monsters and creatures, heavenly punishments, storms, and so on. According to the rule that the myth must be regarded on the subjective level, these companions can be considered as parts of Odysseus'

personality. In this sense, the companions represent still immature and unintegrated mental aspects which, because of their
immaturity, have a strong tendency to regress. Interestingly, the
companions are always sent to address mischief or breaches of
orders when Odysseus is sleeping – thus, when consciousness,
with its strength and focus, is switched off and the total personality finds itself in an unconscious state. Jung referred to this
with a term borrowed from French psychiatry 'abaissment du
niveau mental'. The loss of the companions in the course of
the journey would then be understood psychologically as the
maturing Ego increasingly losing its immaturities and regressive inclinations and achieving an increasing focus and ability
to control its impulses – what in psychoanalysis is called Ego
strength.

In an early episode of the journey, Odysseus' ships land
on an unknown shore, which turns out to be the land of the
lotus eaters. These lotus eaters spend most of their day in a
lotus plant-induced state of intoxication. A group of Odysseus'
companions become addicted to this high and do not return
to the ships. This is an impressive image of regressive tendencies, in this case the tendency to use intoxicating substances
and along with this to lose control of the Ego. In a later episode, the ships dock in a land of cannibals, to whom another
portion of the companions fall victim. These cannibals can
also be considered as a part of the whole personality. They are
the archaic, aggressive side of the personality, whose impulses
can be costly for the Ego if they break through. In the later
episodes, the companions commit a whole series of other errors.
They insult the giant Polyphemus after the ships have successfully escaped from him, and which leads to him throwing rocks
at them and sinking more ships. As they land on the island
of the wind god Aeolus, the companions steal his holy cattle,
despite being forbidden to do so by Odysseus. As punishment
for this, more of them meet their fate in a storm. It is always
Odysseus who manages to escape from the difficult situation
with cunning or an idea, a bold plan or a device. This motif of
the increasing reduction is typical for the individuation process.
The immature elements of the personality fall away and the

conscious parts become stronger and sharper, as if a sculpture was being carved. This makes it clear, moreover, that as a rule the individuation process is a painful process, full of conflicts, losses, and questioning. Its end product is an Ego reduced to its true mass that knows its limitations but has also realised and integrated its inner potential. What is also touched upon in this motif is a basic insight into the individuation process, or about every psychotherapeutic transformation process: it fundamentally cannot happen without a sacrifice. What is meant by this is that the personality must give up on certain aspects in the process of its transformation and self-realisation, for example, grand notions, false self-images, regressive tendencies, and so on. This insight appears in the myth during the journey through the strait of Scylla and Charybdis. Scylla is a monster with multiple heads who takes and absorbs many men from passing ships, and Charybdis is a whirlpool which sucks the ships into an abyss. Odysseus must decide which of these two sides he will choose as a path. He consciously chooses the route past Scylla and consciously sacrifices with this more of his men in order to rescue the others, because otherwise all will be devoured in Charybdis' whirlpool.

Another consistent motif in the Odyssey is the confrontation with and detachment from the archetype of the great mother, which means psychologically speaking, an entanglement with one's own unconscious. It ultimately includes also a detachment from the real entanglement with one's own parental figures and the regression to being a child again. The threatening monsters of the myth, the vortex Charybdis, the cave of Polyphemus, but also the regressive indulgence with the lotus eaters or the cattle of the wind gods, are all ultimately images for the restricting and devouring aspects of the archetype of the great mother. In this way, the myth describes the psychological path of the conscious Ego out of being held in the unconscious and its increasing separation, differentiation, and self-actualisation.

Starting from this differentiation from the mother archetype, the myth finally describes a line of development relating to female figures. These can all be understood as manifestations of the Anima. The first meeting with the Anima happens for

Odysseus when he meets the sorceress Circe. This can be understood as a form of the archaic great goddess, the mistress of
animals. She is a magician and possesses the ability to transform
and to perform magic. Odysseus' companions consequently fall
under her spell and are transformed into pigs, and as such are
reduced to their pure instinctive, primitive nature. Odysseus
now faces the question of how he must deal with this figure.
He receives help here from 'his' goddess, Athena. She advises
him to go to Circe with his sword drawn and then she will let
him have his way with her. This sword can be psychologically
understood as the ability of reason as a conscious function to
decide. If consciousness does not let the mind be lulled by the
magic of the Anima, and thus can resist the regression to the
instinctive nature, although at the same time is able to be open
for its inspiration and to be in contact with it, then consciousness can benefit from the wisdom of the Anima. Here, a certain distinction in the attitude of consciousness faced with the
feminine has taken place. The feminine is no longer effective in
its devouring mother form, but rather animated in a positive
sense. That can only be achieved, however, because consciousness is now so strong that it cannot be pulled into regression,
but rather stays in a relationship and at the same time remains
differentiated. Circe would be, therefore, an image of the Anima
in its alluring and enchanting aspect, which leads the personality into regression and reduces it to its primitive nature. Only
when consciousness can maintain its sharpness and mental fac-
ulties is it in a position to take a stand against this aspect of the
Anima and to profit from it. In the myth, Circe gives Odysseus
advice on how he can shape his journey towards Ithaka. She
warns him of dangers and gives him instructions on how he can
receive important advice by gaining entry to the underworld.
With her help, Odysseus finds the entrance to the underworld
and there meets the blind seer Tiresias, who gives him detailed
instructions on his journey to his homeland. Moreover, he
prophesises for him the loss of all his companions. The blind
prophet Tiresias can be considered as a figure of the Old Sage
with his knowledge, who lies hidden behind the Anima and to
whom contact is only possible when a relationship with the

Anima is established. Psychologically it is a contact between consciousness and the unconscious, so that consciousness can participate in this transcendental knowledge. In order to access Tiresias, Odysseus must take a trip to Okeanos, to the borders of the known world, and must, moreover, psychologically speaking, engage with the deep unconscious, in its aspect of the unknown, non-Ego. The encounter with Teiresias is successful, although the Erebos opens, from which emerge dead souls that harass Odysseus. This can be psychologically understood as the danger of being overpowered by the collective unconscious, what can be described as inflation in analytical psychology and corresponds, clinically speaking, to psychosis. Odysseus can again also prevent this danger through his decisiveness. Here, in the underworld, at Acheron, at the boundary to the kingdom of the dead, it is also the turning point of the *Odyssey*. From here the journey home is described.

In the next episode, after Odysseus and his fellow travellers have left the island of Circe behind them, they travel past the island of the Sirens. These are man-murdering monsters, who possess a wonderful, mesmerising song with which they lure the passing ships to their doom. Again, the bewitching and ultimately devouring aspect of the Anima is presented which, psychologically speaking again, is heavily connected with the devouring aspect of the maternal. Odysseus stuffs the ears of his men with wax on Circe's advice so that the Sirens' song cannot be heard. He, however, would at least like to hear the song once and lets himself be tied to the mast so that he cannot be lured in or give into his impulses. This is also a clear image of the hero aspect of the conscious Ego, which is ready to expose itself to danger, thus opening itself to the influences from the unconscious, and is at the same time in the right condition to control its impulsiveness and its inclination towards regression.

After Odysseus and his companions have finally left behind the challenges of the island of the wind god as well as Scylla and Charybdis, they are finally completely wiped out and destroyed in a storm sent by the sea god Poseidon. Only Odysseus remains and is shipwrecked on the island of the nymph Calypso. The beautiful demi-goddess falls in love with the hero and holds him captive for many years on her island. This is indeed, on the one hand, a state of wonderful love and fulfilment, but nevertheless Odysseus sits sadly on the shore and desires only his homeland. This can be understood psychologically as an image of a danger of the individuation process that the Ego identifies with the inner figures it faces up to. Here it would be the total fusion with the Anima, thus a sinking into the inner world instead of the relationship with a real counterpart. Odysseus appears here again as an image of an individuating consciousness since he desires the real relationship with his wife in place of the nymph's fantasy world. While so far Odysseus has been continually pursued by the sea god Poseidon, who, although masculine, ultimately can be associated with the great mother (of the sea), a gathering of gods in Olympus now decides, out of sympathy for Odysseus, that he may return home. This symbolises the integration of the inner factors, of one's inner archetypal powers, for which the gods stand as symbols. Odysseus can now be released on a raft from the island of Calypso, whereby the archetype of the exposure and extreme threat to the hero, to the individuated Ego, manifests itself. On the way he comes across the Phaiaken, a friendly tribe who offer for him to stay with them and be celebrated as a hero, and Nausicaa, the king's daughter, is offered to him as a bride. This is now a new Anima figure, who is friendly, human, and approachable, but ultimately still represents a manifestation of the inner world. The point here is not to remain attached to the inner image, but to cultivate the relationship with her (Odysseus promises to remember her every day at home and to pray to her like to a goddess), but at the same time to distinguish the real partner from the Anima and to remain faithful to the longing for the Self (home). Odysseus can, therefore, finally return to Ithaca, but finds Penelope surrounded by many suitors who are convinced of Odysseus' death and ask for her hand in marriage. These suitors can also be understood as immature parts of the personality and false self-images from which the personality must cleanse itself in order to successfully arrive home, to the Self, and so that the relationship to the inner figures as well as to the real partner can be realised. Odysseus does finally manage to defeat the suitors by being the only person in a competition who is able to shoot an arrow through a small ring – this is also another image of the focus of consciousness.

The great processes, which from a psychological perspective are thematised in this myth, are the maturation and the differentiation of consciousness, the demarcation from the inner femininity, the Anima, from the archetype of the mother, as well as overcoming archaic and regressive parts of the personality, in the sense of reducing the Ego to its appropriate size. At the end of the myth it seems, however, that the goddess Athena has continually supported Odysseus in this process. Athena, although a female god, is born from the head of Zeus and is an image of the very conscious and rationally oriented feminine aspects of the psyche, in principle the Sophia mentioned above, the personification of feminine wisdom, essentially an image of a unification of opposites. The myth ends with a touching scene in which the goddess Athena reveals herself to Odysseus and explains to him her continual support:

> There the goddess smiled, the bright eyed Athena, and stroked him with her hand and resembled the shape of a woman, beautiful and great, and one who knows wonderful works, and lifted him up and said to him the winged words: he would have to be wise and mischievous, he who wants to try to overtake you in all tricks, and it would have to be a god to stand opposite you, you cunning, thoughtful, insatiable of tricks, and yet did you not recognize Pallas Athena, the daughter of Zeus, I, who was always standing by your side in all hardships and watch over you? The very wise Odysseus then answered her and said: 'Hard is it to recognize you, goddess, for a mortal who meets you, no matter how knowledgeable he may be. For you transform yourself into everything'.
>
> (Weiss 1922, p. 387f)

The myth is also a clear illustration of the always newly emerging problems in the individuation process, in which development only takes place with conflicts that push towards confrontation and becoming conscious. Again and again the Ego must face up to the influences of the unconscious. Ultimately, all of these influences force the transformation towards wholeness.

The archetype of the hero myth

The odyssey outlined here corresponds like many other classical myths and fairy tales with the archetypal basic structure of the hero myth. Jung had already been concerned with this myth even in his earliest publication, *Symbols of Transformation* (Jung CW 5), in which he formulated the concept of archetypes and their effects on the psychotic fantasies of a young woman. Particularly this archetypal, mythical basic structure of the journey of the hero has been dealt with in many different representations in analytical psychology as well as also in neighbouring sciences. The universal structure of the hero myth contains the birth of the hero in poor circumstances, the appearance of exceptional powers and talents in the youth, a quick rise to renown and glory, the successful struggle against the evil antagonists, the susceptibility to exuberance and pride (hubris) due to the hero's outstanding fame, and the homecoming or sacrificial death (Henderson in Jung et al. 1968). The path of the hero illustrates, according to Jung, the development of a person's consciousness, throughout which universal human themes must pervade. Thus, the hero myth symbolises the individuation process, the way to psychological maturation, the development of the individuated Ego consciousness through the confrontation with specific challenges, conflicts, experiences, and one's own unconscious. The hero must, during his adventures, exhibit the power to open himself up to his own unconscious, and the courage, which this journey requires, marks him out as a hero. The letting in of the unconscious as the darkest area of the psyche finds its analogy in the dangerous and unfamiliar places which the hero must break out of during his journey. Following Jung's work, the concept of the journey of the hero as an archetype has been enormously popularised thanks to the publication of the English mythologist Joseph Campbell's (2008) exploration *The Hero with a Thousand Faces*. Borrowing closely from Jung's

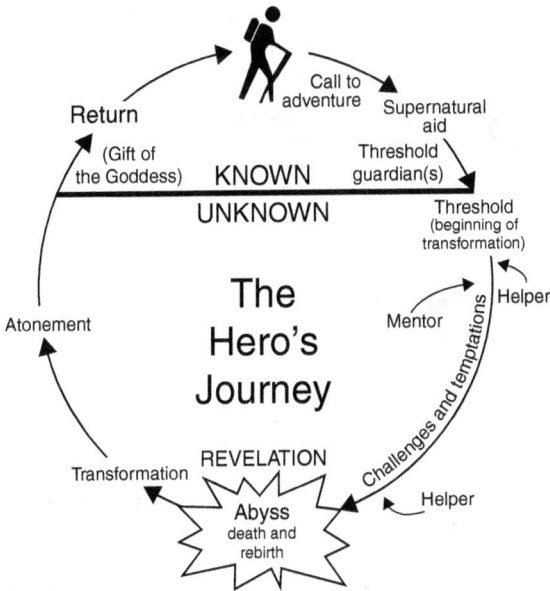

Figure 5.2 'The Journey of the Hero' from Campbell 1999/Wikipedia. org.

conception, he discerns the basic structure of the journey of the hero, as it appears countless in fairy tales and myths from all over the world. This continually recurring basic structure is illustrated in the following diagram:

In the archetypal fundamental pattern of the hero's journey, the hero goes through the following succession of episodes or experiences:

Call and Conflict: The starting point of the hero's journey is frequently a result of a conflict situation or a deficit of some kind. Initially the person, who will later become the hero, receives a call that he must inevitably follow. Normally this involves a challenge from an evil enemy, a monster, or a hostile power which threatens the hero and his people, partly even the whole land or the whole of humanity. The task of the hero is to defeat this threat or to obtain an element or substance which will defend them from or remove the threat. In order to complete this, the hero must set out for a foreign land. Often these foreign places are associated with threats or uncanniness, Campbell calls this place the 'underworld' or the 'nightworld'.

Rejection: Since he must sacrifice his security to start his hero's journey, the hero hesitates to follow the call. The new and unknown makes him fearful, and it is clear how much courage and effort it takes to really set out on the journey.

Departure: The hero overcomes his hesitation and begins his journey. On crossing the threshold, he steps into a world that is foreign, other, and magical to him. This is the beginning of the journey into the darkness.

Supernatural help: As soon as the hero begins to make his way, he encounters a helper or mentor who supports him, who expands his horizon, and confronts him with the challenge and prepares him for it. Moreover, they provide the hero with an elixir, a talisman, or another protective element. In this way they arm and support the hero for the tests which lie ahead.

Tests: Obstacles appear, which can be interpreted as tests. The hero must pass these.

Confrontation and struggle with the adversary: Frequently used motifs for these tests or struggles are: the fight with the dragon or monster (e.g., Siegfried); the killing and dismemberment of the hero (e.g., Osiris); the journey through the night, thus a journey into the darkness, the underworld, or another extreme place – a special variant is exacerbation and a stay in the stomach of the whale (e.g., Jonah). For these tests or struggles the hero receives support from various helpers, for example, entities with magical power or talking animals.

Transformation and Initiation of the hero: At the high point of the journey through the world, the hero discovers the elixir, thus the solution to the initial challenge. The overpowering and evil opponent, the dragon, is vanquished. Frequently this is only achieved after the hero has been in a serious condition of peril or despair, is completely exposed. He is a hero precisely in that he is alone. The hero shows fear and trepidation, and only by the hero letting go of his old behaviours and experiences can he mobilise all his power and defeat this evil. A frequently used additional element is the freeing of the imprisoned maiden and the wedding which follows. In this stage the hero acquires the valuable treasure that could rescue their world. Often, the hero recognises his true life's meaning as he conquers the evil, which is the real profit of the treasure.

Denial of the return journey: Although the hero has passed the greatest test in the underworld, he hesitates to return to the normal world. This often seems to be an escape from responsibility in the original world (e.g., Ulysses stays with Calypso, although Penelope has been waiting for him for years and is harassed by suitors).

Release from the underworld and crossing the threshold: The hero decides to begin his return journey and go back to the world he is used to. On the brink of this, another challenge arises which can be characterised as a rescue and re-evaluation of the hero after a battle at the threshold. Often, yet another difficulty appears here, because the hero is initially met with incomprehension or disbelief (fight with the suitors). The task is now to integrate the successes of the journey into the normal reality.

Return and the 'lord of two worlds': After the return to his departure point as the new 'lord of two worlds', who has mastered the initial threat and challenge, typically the hero then replaces the previous ruler, king and so on. The hero now knows both worlds and can guide and support unexperienced initiates. He has successfully integrated his newly acquired knowledge in this side of reality and the community profits from his wisdom.

In his expansive work, Campbell has given evidence of this basic structure in numerous fairy tales and myths from the most different cultures and time periods. Furthermore, Campbell gives fundamental consideration to the creation of myths.

> In every mythological system that has been spread throughout the long history and prehistory in the different zones and areas of the world, these two basic insights – the inevitability of death and the permanence of societal order – are symbolically connected with each other and thus form the factor which shapes the embryonic rites and consequently the society.
>
> (1991, p. 30)

Campbell assigns four basic functions to myths with this basic structure:

The mystic function: The focal point here is waking the consciousness of man and his everyday understanding with the 'Mysterium tremendum et fascinans' of the cosmos.

The cosmological function: Through the clear basic structure, the myth provides an overall picture of the universe. In opposition to the sciences, which attempt to give an exact description of the universe, the myth only provides a meaningful and explanatory figure of the mystery behind all things.

The societal function: In the myths, societies and human communities have laid down basic social orders in narrative form. Through the tradition of the myth, this basic order is transmitted to the individuals in the society and the basic order itself is ever more engraved in the history of the people or the community. In this sense, the myths explain an ethical function of how life in a good community should be meaningfully organised.

The pedagogical function: The reason for the telling and handing down of myths is first and foremost to educate individuals so that they come into harmony with themselves, their culture, and the macrocosm. In this sense the myths convey even in the early human communities a basic order of what it means to lead a human life and, in this sense, had a central orientation function for social coexistence.

With this argument, Campbell goes slightly further than Jung by not only engaging with the individual psychological meaning of the myth, but also taking a sociocultural and anthropological perspective, what Jung had only done in a rudimental way. Campbell's publication has gained almost as much popularity as Jung's original concept in the cultural sciences, as will be made clear in the following example of the reception of film productions. Campbell has always explicitly related his work to that of Jung and his archetype theory.

FEATURE FILM – THE MYTHS OF LATE MODERNITY

Investigating mythological narratives for their underlying structure has proved itself to be an extremely productive approach in cultural studies. It could be argued, however, that this is less relevant for modern people, because hardly anyone is concerned with the ancient myths or archaic fairy tales. What follows will show that archetypal narrative structures determine the collective imagination just as before, but these have today taken on other forms of representation, namely that of film. In recent years it has been a popular topic not only in analytical psychology, but also in psychology and psychoanalysis more generally, to consider cinematic films from a depth psychological perspective (Gerlach & Pop 2012, Döring & Möller 2008, Laszig 2013). Motion pictures can be considered as similar to fairy tales and myths as archetypal narratives staged in pictures, which attract an audience of millions precisely because they deal with general human problems and their solutions. At least in Western culture, they are probably for people in general a much more frequently used cultural form than classical myths and fairy tales.

Film has proved itself to be a particularly suited medium of representing the myths of humanity, stories of heroes' development, and also historical crises and how they are overcome. Film frequently takes on the function of fairy tales, in which more individual and family destinies are portrayed in an exemplary manner, especially crises in biographical development, especially adolescence.

(Hirsch 2008, p. 9)

Everyone knows the experience of being strongly emotionally affected by a film, when the experiences of characters move us so much that we take our concern with the events or figures of the film into our daily lives or into our relationships, and it's not rare for this to lead to us making progress in dealing with problems or internal issues or even finding a solution. The ancient philosopher Aristotle describes the cathartic effect of participating in a story – in this case it related to the theatre. The ancient theatre was directly oriented around invoking such an effect in the spectators and in this way contributing to social education and to overcoming difficult emotional problems.

Modern media reception research has been intensely concerned in recent years with why individuals respond particularly strongly to certain media content. In what follows, the concept of 'thematic preoccupation' shall be outlined, which draws on Lorenzer's (1986) approach of a social science psychoanalysis of organising memories, needs, and the unconscious representations of the subject's interactions in the form of images or describing them as scenes or situations. The needs that determine how the media is received are regarded as scenically composed themes, which are recognised in the media narratives in an interpretative way when the media is received and can be extracted to deal with one's own problems and to reassure oneself and construct identity. The recipients are provided with a sort of plot to structure their own inner (unconscious) themes from the media narratives. The scenic representation of the fabric of interactions and relationships in the media leads, moreover, to the recipients identifying with the roles of these media figures, in which a form of identity negotiation takes place through a confrontation with possible behaviour presented in the media. As part of this, consistent behaviour patterns in certain situations and the person's own themes and culturally transmitted forms of action and coping mechanisms can be tested in the fantasy and potentially adopted in one's own behaviour. Popular myths, it is argued, in the form of film stories, describe important human needs, practical experiences, and moral aims. They express human experience, represent feelings and life relationships. Ultimately, they represent the objectification of social experience. The scenic arrangements of mythical patterns in the media can depict the unconscious and similarly action-oriented practical figures of individuals as general basic patterns of experience. In these patterns of social experience processed by the media individuals can reflect and process their own experiences, as they illustrate the unconscious figures in genre and narrative conventions and connect with the mythical narratives via references to other media texts. This is what, at least, modern media theory argues. Using Jung's ideas, we can also add that the unconscious themes, with which the recipients are concerned, follow archetypal basic structures, and that if these are recognised in the narrative of the media, the audience will experience a sense of identifying with these narratives and therefore become emotionally involved. Moreover, if the media narrative fully depicts the archetypal pattern, this also contains development potential according to the dynamics of the archetype beyond just the situation of the individual which are aimed towards wholeness. This also makes the fascination of late-modern societies with media narratives understandable. In principle, the interest of one person in a certain film can be used in psychotherapy in very similar ways to the classic approaches using a fairy tale or myth. That modern film productions contain the same archetypal narrative structures as the classical fairy tales and myths will now be made clear through analysis of an example.

AN EXEMPLARY ANALYSIS: JAMES BOND – THE MODERN HERO

If we consider the most successful action films in recent years (e.g., the *Bourne* series, *Mission Impossible*, *Die Hard*, *James Bond*), it becomes apparent that all of these productions follow a very similar narrative scheme, which corresponds with the archetype of the hero narrative. The structural characteristics of this narrative structure have already been detailed above, but here are a few additional notes to consider:

1   The narrative is defined by a conflict or opposition, the confirmation of the protagonist as a hero in the struggle against a negative opponent with the aim of overcoming them.
2   This opponent is, at least at the beginning, superior; the struggle appearing to be hopeless is precisely what makes it heroic. The task of the hero seems impossible, and he or she will have to make the impossible possible (*Mission Impossible*) in order to achieve his or her goal.
3   In his or her struggle, the hero is either consistently, or at least partly, completely alone (e.g., radio contact is lost, the hero is separated from his team, the weapons malfunction, and so on). This matches the element of the exposure of the hero archetype.
4   Along with this exposure, there is also, however, a figure who helps the hero and provides things that are essential for the action; in the late-modern era this is above all technological help.
5   The hero does not act in his or her own interest, but instead works towards a higher goal, to rescue mankind, potentially sacrificing him- or herself, or at the very least to putting his or her own life at risk ('For England!').
6   The hero fights for something right and just, while the opponent is the representative of an unjust, morally inferior, or historically redundant cause.

An excellent example containing all of these elements is the *James Bond* film series, which has recently celebrated its fiftieth anniversary. If the films of the series are analysed, the narrative structure presented above can consistently be found. The hero, James Bond, is a modern knight. He is impeccably dressed with perfect manners, the personification of a gentleman, gallant to women, and fearless in conflict with his enemies. He does not usually fight for anything other than to save the world and, in line with this, his opponents have from the beginning something monstrous about them, a deformation or even mythical powers (e.g., the famous 'Jaws' – this corresponds to the ogre or dragon of a myth). There is never any doubt that the villains are evil through and through and normally plan to destroy the world. In all the films of the series, the plot is formed around the process of dealing with a situation in which Bond sees himself alone against the opponents, isolated and exposed, and his struggle appears to be desperate in light of the superiority of the opponent (exposure). Never, however, does he give up or let his hope fade away. In the direst situations, some helpers come to his side, most notably the leader of the research and development division, 'Q' (miraculous helper). At precisely the right time, he can rescue Bond from his situation with a new technological device and allow him to triumph in his final fight against evil. In order to do this, Bond must frequently go down into the hellish structures of his opponents (night sea journey). Along with rescuing the world, Bond must also, in all films, always save a beautiful woman, the notorious Bond girl (Anima), who is sure to have been captured by the enemy. Bond must liberate the beautiful woman while saving the world (the imprisoned maiden). At the start this seems impossible, but Bond makes the impossible possible, overcomes the enemy, frees the woman, and comes together with her at the end (divine union).

Even if the story appears in the guise of the late-modern period and it is no longer about knights and dragons, but rather agents and arms dealers, the structure of the hero myth has, in itself, not changed. Considered from a psychological perspective, the archetype of the hero narrative describes the path of development of an initially weak Ego, which frees itself from the clutches of unconscious powers, for example, an inferiority complex, in an arduous struggle in order to be able to control its own life with the acquired power and to become capable of having a relationship. The hero's evil opponents embody the repressive powers in one's own psyche which prevent the Ego from being autonomous and functioning unimpededly in the world. The beautiful woman, however, can be seen as a personification of the relationship to one's own psyche and the capacity to have a relationship in general. It is, therefore, possible to assume that it is precisely those people, supposedly young people, who are still in the process of developing the strength of their Ego and breaking away from both the personal ties of childhood and the unconscious attachment to childhood needs and fears, who are attracted to this myth. This myth has lost none of its relevance or attractiveness for individuals in the late-modern period. Successful film producers and directors understand how to use such narrative structures and to give them new shapes in their films. We could suspect that scriptwriters and directors of successful modern films draw on their intuitive knowledge of the archetypal narrative structures and incorporate these into their modern film productions and, because the archetypal structures speak to many people emotionally, these films gain a huge following. This is surely so in many cases and corresponds with the understanding of the artist in analytical psychology, who has special access to the archetypal basic pattern of the soul and can bring this to bear in artistic forms. Astoundingly, the film industry, or at least Hollywood, targeted very early on the psychological understanding of narratives structures and drew on certain narrative structures and also explicitly on Jung's theories of the myth of the hero and its psychological significance. The author Christopher Vogler has been regarded for decades as one of the most well-known university tutors for screenwriters and mentors for screenwriters from the large production companies in Hollywood. In his handbook for film composition, *The Odyssey of the Screenwriter* (Vogler 1997), he draws explicitly on the classic work of Joseph Campbell, *The Hero with a Thousand Faces*. Vogler shows how this basic pattern of the hero myth can be used as a blueprint for the development of screenplays. He exemplifies this fundamental structure in a series of modern motion pictures, including *Titanic*, *Pulp Fiction*, *The Lion King*, and finally the series *Star Wars*.

The educational scientist Walden (2015) also follows in his interpretation of so-called blockbuster films, meaning Hollywood productions which are extraordinarily successful, the approach that Campbell had set down in his structure of the hero's journey. His thesis is that the successful films that come out of Hollywood speak to many people and are particularly economically successful precisely because they follow the archetypal structure of the hero's journey and in this way speak to people unconsciously. Based on a detailed interpretation of primarily the first films in the *Star Wars* saga, he can convincingly demonstrate the implicit use of the structure of the hero's journey in this modern motion picture.

The hero in this science fiction saga is the young Luke Skywalker, who, like every hero, appears to be naive and inexperienced at the start. He receives his calling through a hologram, which is transmitted by two robots, who have landed on his planet fleeing from the troops of the evil empire. In this hologram, a message to Obi-Wan Kenobi from Princess Leia is transmitted to him. This old Jedi Knight represents, then, the teacher and mentor for young Luke who guides and supports him in his task of fighting against the empire. Whilst putting together a group, Luke visits a spaceport on the planet Tatooine – this location symbolises the archetypal threshold where the hero now changes from his usual world into the world of dragon fighting. There Luke can hire the talented space pilot Han Solo, with whom he flees Tatooine and makes it to the inside of the Death Star. Inside the Death Star the group splits up; Luke sets his sights on freeing the imprisoned princess (maiden), while Obi-Wan Kenobi does battle with the dark lord Darth Vader, his former pupil. This represents the high point or climax in the hero's journey, at which point the mentor loses his life. Luke manages, however, to rescue the princess and they flee together from the Death Star. At the end of the hero's journey, Luke fights with the rebels against the empire around the Death Star and after the normal difficulties he is successful in destroying the Death Star. The hero and his people land on a neighbouring planet, on which the fighters are honoured and which likewise means the return to usual daily life (detailed in Walden 2015).

Interestingly, we can see evidence that George Lucas explicitly takes Campbell's myth research into account:

I carry out studies to distil the narratives which are universal to all myths. I attribute the success [of *Star Wars*] more than anything to the psychological underpinning that has been there for thousands of years. People react precisely as they have done to stories in the past. I wanted to make a film that promotes the contemporary mythology and simultaneously heralds a new type of moral. No-one really gets to the bottom of it; we are always content with some abstract explanation. No one says to the kids of today: hey, listen, that is right and that is wrong.

> (from an interview with the director George Lucas
> and Bill Moyers, quoted in Walden 2015, p. 75ff)

5.3.2 Archetypes in political psychology

In Jung's approaches for analysing collective processes, a sort of social psychology (what Jung described as 'mass psychology') can be found in the use of the archetype concept (Jung, CW 10). Thus, Jung had concerned himself with the emerging National Socialism and its use of old Germanic myths and symbols in political agitation. The archetype concept is extremely useful in making clear and explaining how political propaganda successfully emotionally mobilises a huge number of people using archetypal elements, even for intensely irrational goals. Political phenomena like anti-Semitism or general xenophobia can be interpreted as a collective projection of the archetypal shadow onto certain population groups. Unfortunately, there have been up until now very few systematic attempts in analytical psychology to make the archetype concept useful in the sense of a political psychology and to understand political processes against the background of archetypes (Zoja 2002, 2009). As an example of this approach being put into practice, we can consider the contemporary political situation in the USA against the background of a mythical scheme. In Anglo-American literature, an archetypal narrative, a version of the hero myth, the so-called 'American Monomyth' has been discussed for a long time (Lawrence & Jewett 2002). This mythical narrative, as many authors have shown, stretches throughout the literary imagination and the artistic achievements in literature, poetry, and recently film production in the USA since the time of the colonialists in the seventeenth century right through to modern film productions. Typically, this narrative begins in an idyllic, sheltered community of settlers living peacefully with one another and working on the land. This community is essentially depicted as good and free from argument and conflict. An evil enemy from outside forces its way into this idyllic community and threatens the existence of the whole community. The institutions of the state, usually presented as democratic, are not aware of this threat and fail, also because they prove themselves to be incompetent or corrupt. In this situation a heroic, male figure emerges, who stands alone against this threatening enemy and in doing so overrides democratic institutions and the rule of law. Only with brute force does this hero succeed in overcoming the threat and restoring the initial paradisiacal state, which he ultimately does not take part in, disappearing once again into nowhere. In the discussion of this monomyth, it will be shown in detail how this narrative has developed out of the experience of the first settlers on the border to wilderness, in the reclamation of the landscape and the struggle for civilisation, always under the threat of the European colonial powers. From the earliest narratives of the Puritans, which are still completely influenced by their confrontation with the indigenous Indian population, through the typical Western stories of the nineteenth and early twentieth centuries up to the film production of the Hollywood industry, the decisive influence of this myth can be proven. Interestingly, the story's narrative stands in stark contrast to America's official political self-image as the home of democracy, since the narrative legitimises the superhero resorting to authoritarian leadership, ruthless violence, vigilante justice, and hateful revenge, due to the failure of state law and order. This is very clearly a narrative pattern with an archetypal character, a variant of the hero myth. Interestingly, this has had an enormous influence on real American politics in the last two centuries. The attacks of September 11 fatally corresponded, at least as they have been interpreted and read by the media, with the mythical narrative of the sudden intrusion of evil into the peaceful, idyllic community. In its course of action, the Bush administration also drew on the monomyth in an almost perfidious manner: the enemy was demonised as 'the axis of evil'. This legitimated not only the invasion of

Afghanistan and Iraq – in the case of the latter, the violation of international law could only be covered up with falsified evidence of alleged weapons of mass destruction – but also drone warfare, which is still outside international law. The political rhetoric used in this way is consistent with the juxtaposition of the enemy demonised as evil and the goal of bringing freedom and democracy to all peoples of the world, and thus matches precisely the archetypal scheme of the struggle of the civilisation on the boundaries of the wilderness. Not only the political rhetoric, however, follows the monomyth so extensively, but also the media's staging draws on archetypal patterns, without knowledge of which the form of political action would appear highly irrational and would be difficult to comprehend. A striking example of this is the media staging of President George W. Bush's declaration of "mission accomplished" in the war against Iraq on an American aircraft carrier. The footage that was made available to the media, cut and edited by the Pentagon, suggests that the president had single-handedly flown a fighter jet and landed on the aircraft carrier. The image gives the impression of him as having come over the vastness of the Pacific from out of nowhere. Actually, as has been previously openly stated in American reports, the aircraft carrier lay only a few kilometres from the California coast, but the camera angle was always directed towards the wide Pacific Ocean. Bush had of course not flown the plane himself, but this had been cut out. In the film footage he is only seen getting out of the aircraft, taking off his helmet, being received by the jubilant congregation, and announcing in a theatrical pose the termination of the assault on Iraq. If we consider this staging against the background of the archetypal hero myth, we can see that the decisive part of the staging is that the rescuing superhero comes from outside into the community threatened by evil and must take the fight to the enemy alone and by himself. As disconcerting and downright ridiculous as such a staging must appear to the informed observer, it cannot be denied that the power of this for political mobilisation was enormous. It helped the USA politically justify the invasion of Iraq to a population still sceptical about the traumas in Vietnam and Somalia, as the war was given a mythical aura by the characterisation: 'We, the good, bring freedom and democracy to peoples enslaved by evil'.

This example can illustrate the enormous impact that the targeted use of archetypal patterns and mythical narratives can have in politics. In the era of Donald Trump, the use of the myth has reached a climax, since he was successful in the election as an alleged 'outsider' who would clean up with 'the system' – which is of course ridiculous because probably nobody is so much part of the establishment as Trump. And again we see the pattern of the political system being characterised as rotten and evil, which justifies the overriding of democratic and legal institutions. Also, the power of the archetypal narrative to distort reality and create 'alternative facts' ('myths') has become frightening. The example given here, of course, tends to show the potentially destructive character of these archetypes. The commitment of Mahatma Gandhi on the path to India's independence from Britain would be an example of the humane side of the impact of archetypal structures. There is no doubt, however, that archetypal structures can be demonstrated in numerous political strategies, and it can be argued that it is precisely these that give politics its power of mobilisation.

6 What is the state of archetype theory?

A tentative conclusion

It is clear, particularly in the depiction of the different fields in which archetype theory can be used, that it not only finds wide (and effective) usage in the clinical field, but is also accepted in the cultural sciences and has even achieved a currency there. In the cultural sciences, in particular in literary studies and its most recent form, film theory (Bassil-Morozow & Hockley 2016, Hauke & Allister 2001), as well as in the areas of theology and religious studies, Jung's archetype theory has been even more strongly received than many Jungians are aware of. That is only one side of the story. The overview of the research has shown that the classical concept of the transmission of archetypes as Jung and his direct students conceived of it is not tenable when considered alongside the most up-to-date knowledge in life sciences. In this sense archetype theory is an area for development. Central parts of the classical concept, like the idea of genetic transmission from generation to generation, the idea of universality, and also the extent of what can be taken as archetypal, are fundamentally in question. Although this has been increasingly discussed since the end of the 1990s, in particularly in Anglo-American literature (above all the *Journal of Analytical Psychology* as the central forum of discussion), neither practitioners nor educational structures have taken this enough into account. In Jungian publications, Jung's classical argumentation can still be found unquestioned. As an engaged observer of Jungian literature, it is also possible to get the impression that if authors are concerned with new

DOI: 10.4324/9781003058458-6

knowledge, for example, from neuroscience, this knowledge is so selectively dealt with that it ultimately repeats the outdated views of archetype theory. For the view of an outside observer who is informed about the state of scientific knowledge, such as a biologist, ethnologist, or psychiatrist, archetype theory must appear as a field of rubble. If at present, the classical Jungian ideas of how alleged archetypal patterns are passed from generation to generation in such a way that their universality is assured for all people in all cultures, is by no means backed by contemporary scientific insight, then archetype theory as a central building block of analytical psychology is questionable.

On the other hand, the concept can be productively worked with in clinical environments as well as in the analysis of cultural phenomena. The situation of the fragmented basic theory is also in no way exclusive to analytical psychology. In medicine, for example, many treatment methods are effectively employed, although nothing or only very little is known about their working mechanisms. One of Jung's classic case studies can be regarded afresh against this background (in 'The Structure of the Psyche', Jung CW 8). It relates to a case of an army officer who came to therapy with various hysterical conversion symptoms. Some central symptoms were able to be resolved by making conscious the emotions which had been unconscious up until that point. There remained, however, an organically inexplicable pain in the patient's heel. The patient then had a dream in which he was bitten in the heel by a snake and was immediately paralysed. Here, Jung makes archetypal references to the symbol of the snake bite in the heel. Merchant (2012), however, discusses the case in light of the emergence theory mentioned above and demonstrates that the case and the dream symbol can be interpreted without any reference to genuinely archetypal elements in the sense of spontaneously occurring, previously completely unconscious stocks of knowledge. The patient had a dominant and overprotective mother, which led to him remaining dependent and his masculinity being less developed. To compensate for this, in his early adulthood he turned in completely the opposite direction and joined the army, where he covered up his weakness with military might. Merchant argues here that the image of being bitten in the heel by a snake can be understood as an expression of the paralysis of the mother's overprotectiveness, which corresponds to an unconscious, archaic thinking about the above-mentioned image pattern. What is decisive here is that the unconscious image does not necessarily have to be archetypal in the sense that it has never been present in the patient's experience. It is also quite possible to argue that this image has formed in the patient's unconscious experience during his development in the experience with the mother as a form of archaic consolidation.

A tentative conclusion to the archetype theory would be, therefore, that we can work as before in the clinical practice in the ways depicted above and can understand archetypal images as forms of subconscious adaptation of psychic processes, without necessarily recalling that these images come from a collective unconscious that was never part of the person's experience.

However, I think that in light of the findings presented here, we should be more cautious about asserting the universality of archetypes. As I have tried to show, the more complex archetypes, in the sense of process structures that can be represented in narrative form, seem to be mediated much more through social-isation and enculturation than through biological means. The socialisation processes, however, are prone to failure, and there-fore it must be considered that not all humans have access to the complete set of archetypal structures. This could in turn explain why some courses of clinical therapies are ineffective or even fail, and why some patients present no symbols or other references to archetypal structures and do not benefit from the Jungian treatment. A plausible explanation here would be that they are not able to establish a connection to these archetypal structures because they simply do not have them.

My recommendation to the analytical psychology commu-nity in this position would be to concern itself in the future intensely with socialisation processes as ways of transferring archetypal structures. This would also enable the archetype concept to connect with current concepts such as the theory of memes (Wilson 2012). Parallel to genes as the biological substrate of information that is passed on from generation to generation, memes are conceptualised as stocks of knowledge that have a place in the collective knowledge stock of a culture and are, so to speak, passed on from generation to generation in cultural memory. A similar concept already existed with the science theorist Karl Popper at the end of the 1920s in his so-called 3-worlds concept. The third world comprises, as Popper puts it, 'objective knowledge' that exists in a culture at a certain time, independent of the cognitive states of individuals (and thus bears great resemblance to Jung's concept of the 'objective psyche'). This would allow an interesting reconception of the collective unconscious as a collective memory of humanity independent of biological claims. Likewise, the investigation of the completely unconscious level of interaction between therapist and patient, the so-called interactive field, seems to me to be a promising possibility for a better understanding of the processes that lead to therapeutic change through the activation of archetypal patterns. There are now various indications that much more interaction takes place at this level and much more complex information is conveyed than previously thought possible (Gödde & Buchholz 2011 overview in Roesler 2013).

The debate about the theory of archetypes remains exciting. On the one hand, Jung has made an extremely important discovery here, which has had a lasting impact not only on psychology but also on other sciences. On the other hand, archetype theory, at least in its present form, cannot be maintained and requires a comprehensive revision. The question is whether those using or practicing analytical psychology can possibly bid farewell to concepts that have become dear to them, or are prepared to change them in such a way that they can find their appropriate place in contemporary sciences.

Appendix

Archetypal Symbol Inventory (from Rosen et al. 1991, pp. 226–227)

Archetypal Symbol Inventory (ASI)

1. Ascent

2. Beauty

3. Birth

4. Center

5. Charity

6. Completion

7. Earth

8. Eternity

9. Evil

10. Feminine

11. Fertility

12. Generativity

13. Harmony

14. Health

15. Knowledge

16. Life

17. Masculine

18. Origin

19. Paradox

20. Perfection

ASI (continued)

21.		Possibility	31.		Sleep
22.		Potential	32.		Soul
23.		Power	33.		Spirit
24.		Progress	34.		Synthesis
25.		Protection	35.		Transformation
26.		Purify	36.		Unconscious
27.		Quest	37.		Unity
28.		Rationality	38.		Valor
29.		Salvation	39.		Virility
30.		Self	30.		Wrath

References

Aarne, A., & Thompson, S. (1964). *The types of the folktale. A classification and bibliography.* Helsinki: Acad. Scient. Fenn.

Adam, K.-U. (2000). *Therapeutisches Arbeiten mit Träumen: Theorie und Praxis der Traumarbeit.* Berlin, Heidelberg: Springer.

Ahnert, L. (2010). *Wieviel Mutter braucht ein Kind?* Heidelberg: Spektrum.

Alexopoulou, A. (2008). *Using 'Archetypal Family Therapy' for meta-analyzing family therapy procedures applied in single parent families of depressed children.* [Unpublished master's thesis]. University of Essex, UK.

Archive for Research in Archetypal Symbolism (ARAS) (2011). *Das Buch der Symbole. Betrachtungen zu archetypischen Bildern.* Köln: Taschen.

Asper, K. (1989). *Verlassenheit und Selbstentfremdung: neue Zugänge zum therapeutischen Verständnis.* Olten: Walter.

Atmanspacher, H. (Hrsg.) (1995). *Der Pauli-Jung-Dialog und seine Bedeutung für die moderne Wissenschaft.* Heidelberg: Springer.

Atmanspacher, H. (2014). 20th century variants of dual-aspect thinking (with commentaries and replies). *Mind and Matter, 12*(2), 245–288.

Atmanspacher, H., & Fach, W. (2013). A structural-phenomenological typology of mind-matter correlations. *Journal of Analytical Psychology, 58*, 219–244.

Atmanspacher, H., Römer, H., & Walach, H. (2002). Weak quantum theory: Complementarity and entanglement in physics and beyond. *Foundations of Physics, 32*, 379–406.

Bächtold-Stäubli, H. (Hrsg.) (2000). *Handwörterbuch des deutschen Aberglaubens.* Berlin: Walter de Gruyter.

Bair, D. (2003). *Jung. A biography.* New York, Boston: Little, Brown.

Baranger, M., & Baranger, W. (2009). *The work of confluence. Listening and interpreting in the psychoanalytic field.* London: Karnac.

Bash, K. W. (1988). *Die analytische Psychologie im Umfeld der Wissenschaften.* Bern: Huber.

Bassil-Morozow H., & Hockley, L. (2016). *Jungian film studies: The essential guide.* London: Routledge.

Bastian, A. (1881). *Der Völkergedanke im Aufbau einer Wissenschaft vom Menschen.* Berlin: Dietrich Reimer.

Bauer, J. (2002). *Das Gedächtnis des Körpers. Wie Beziehungen und Lebensstile unsere Gene steuern.* Frankfurt/M.: Eichborn.

Bauer, J. (2005). *Warum ich fühle, was du fühlst: intuitive Kommunikation und das Geheimnis der Spiegelneurone.* Hamburg: Hoffmann und Campe.

Bauer, J. (2006). *Prinzip Menschlichkeit. Warum wir von Natur aus kooperieren.* Hamburg: Hoffmann und Campe.

Bauer, J. (2008). *Das Kooperative Gen. Abschied vom Darwinismus.* Hamburg: Hoffmann und Campe.

Baumgardt, U. (1987). *König Drosselbart und Cg Jungs Frauenbild. Kritische Gedanken zu an immer und animus.* Olten: Walter.

Belsky, J., & Pluess, M. (2009). The nature (and nurture?) of plasticity in early human development. *Perspectives on Psychological Science, 4,* 345–351.

Betz, O. (1989). *Das Geheimnis der Zahlen.* Stuttgart: Kreuz.

Bischof, N. (1996). *Das Kraftfeld der Mythen.* München: Piper.

Bly, R. (1990). *Iron John. A book about men.* New York: Addison-Wesley.

Bolen, J. S. (1984). *Goddesses in Everywoman.* New York: Harper.

Bolen, J. S. (1989). *Gods in Everyman.* New York: Harper and Row.

Boyd, R. D. (1991). *Personal transformations in small groups. A Jungian perspective.* London: Routledge.

Brosse, J. (1992). *Magie der Pflanzen.* Olten: Walter.

Brosse, J. (1994). *Mythologie der Bäume.* Solothurn: Walter.

Buchholz, M. (2005). *Das Unbewusste – ein Pojekt in drei Bänden.* Gießen: Psychosozial.

Buiting, K. (2005). Epigenetische Vererbung. *Medizinische Genetik, 17,* 292–295.

Campbell, J. (2008). *Hero with a thousand faces.* San Francisco: New World Library.

Cassidy, J., & Shaver, P. R. (2018). *Handbook of attachment. Theory, research and clinical applications* (3rd ed.). New York, London: Guilford.

Cassirer, E. (1955). *The philosophy of symbolic forms*. New Haven, London: Yale University Press.

Chomsky, N. (1978). *Topics in the theory of generative grammar*. Den Haag: Mouton.

Collins, F. S. (2011). *The language of life. DNA and the revolution of personalized medicine*. New York: Harper Collins.

Cooper, J. C. (1986). *Illustriertes Lexikon der traditionellen Symbole*. Wiesbaden: Drei Lilien.

Dench, L. N. (2007). *Female athletes' perceptions of archetypology and typology*. [Unpublished doctoral dissertation]. Temple University. Philadelphia.

Dicks, H. V. (1967). *Marital tensions. Clinical studies towards a psychoanalytic theory of interaction*. London: Routledge and Kegan Paul.

Doering, S., & Möller, H. (2008). *Frankenstein und Belle de Jour: 30 Filmcharaktere und ihre psychischen Störungen*. Berlin, Heidelberg: Springer.

Dorst, B. (2014). Symbole als Grundlage der aktiven Imagination. In B. Dorst & R. T. Vogel (Hrsg.). *Aktive Imagination. Schöpferisches Leben aus inneren Bildern* (pp. 51–68). Stuttgart: Kohlhammer.

Drewermann, E. (1984). *Tiefenpsychologie und Exegese*. München: dtv.

Drewermann, E. (2003). *Das Johannes Evangelium*. Düsseldorf: Patmos.

Edinger, E. (1994): *The eternal drama. The inner meaning of Greek mythology*. Boston, London: Shambhala.

Eibl-Eibesfeldt, I. (1987). *Grundriß der vergleichenden Verhaltensforschung*: München: Piper.

Eisenstädter, J. (1912). *Elementargedanke und Übertragungstheorie in der Völkerkunde*. Stuttgart: Strecker & Schröder.

Ekman, P., Friesen, W., O'Sullivan, M., & Chan, A. (1987). Universals and cultural differences in the judgment of facial expressions of emotions. *Journal of Personality and Social Psychology, 53*, 712–717.

Eschenbach, U. (1986). *Die Behandlung in der Analytischen Psychologie*. Stuttgart: Bonz.

Fine, C. (2010). *Delusions of gender: The real science behind sex differences*. New York: Norton.

Freud, S. (1933). Neue Folge der Vorlesungen zur Einführung in die Psychoanalyse. *GW 15*. Frankfurt/M.: Fischer.

Freud, S. (1939). Der Mann Moses und die monotheistische Religion. *GW 16*. Frankfurt/M.: Fischer.

Freud, S., & Jung, C. G. (1974). *Briefwechsel*. Hrsg. V. W. McGuire u. W. Sauerländer. Frankfurt/M.: Fischer.

Frick, E. (1996). *Durch Verwundung heilen. Zur Psychoanalyse des Heilungsarchetyps.* Göttingen, Zürich: Vandenhoeck und Ruprecht.

Gallese, V. (2003). The roots of empathy: The shared manifold hypothesis and the neural basis of intersubjectivity. *Psychopathology, 36,* 171–180.

Gergen, M. M. (1996). The social construction of personal histories: Gendered lives in popular autobiographies. In T. A. Sarbin & J. I. Kitsuse (Eds.). *Constructing the social* (pp. 18–44). London: SAGE.

Gerlach, A., & Pop, C. (Hrsg.) (2012). *Filmräume – Leinwandträume. Psychoanalytische Filminterpretationen.* Gießen: Psychosozial.

Gödde, G., & Buchholz, M. B. (2011). *Unbewusstes.* Gießen: Psychosozial.

Goodmann, F. (1992). *Trance – der uralte Weg zum religiösen Erleben. Rituelle Körperhaltungen und ekstatische Erlebnisse.* Gütersloh: Gütersloher.

Grof, S. (1978). *Topographie des Unbewussten: LSD im Dienst der tiefenpsychologischen Forschung.* Stuttgart: Klett-Cotta.

Habermas, J. (1968). *Erkenntnis und Interesse.* Frankfurt/M.: Suhrkamp.

Hampe, B. (2005). *From perception to meaning: Image schemas in cognitive linguistics.* New York: Mouton de Gruyter.

Hauke C., & Alister, I. (2001). *Jung and film: Post-Jungian takes on the moving image.* London: Routledge.

Haule, J. R. (2004). *Divine madness: Archetypes of romantic love.* Shiatook: Fisher King Press.

Haule, J. R. (2010). *Jung in the 21st century.* Vol. 1: *Evolution and archetype.* London: Routledge.

Heisig, D. (1996). *Die Anima. Der Archetyp des Lebendigen.* Zürich: Walter.

Henderson, J. (1991). C. G. Jung's psychology: Additions and extensions. *Journal of Analytical Psychology, 36,* 429–442.

Hendricks-Jansen, H. (1996). *Catching ourselves in the act: Situated activity, interactive emergence, evolution and human thought.* Cambridge, MA: MIT Press.

Hillman, J. (1971). *The myth of analysis.* Evanston, IL: Northwestern University Press.

Hillman, J. (1975). *Revisioning psychology.* New York: Harper & Row.

Hillman, J. (1979). *The dream and the underworld.* New York: Harper & Row.

Hillman, J. (1981a). Anima I. *Gorgo, 5,* 45–81.

Hillman, J. (1981b). Anima II. *Gorgo, 6*, 56–89.

Hillman, J. (1983). *Archetypal psychology: A brief account*. Dallas: Spring.

Hillman, J. (1997). *The soul's code*. London: Grand Central Publishing.

Hinterberger, T., & Anton, A. (2012). Die telepathische Verbundenheit der Gehirne – Ergebnisse dreier EEG-Studien mit simultaner Aufzeichnung. In W. Ambach (Hrsg.). *Experimentelle Psychophysiologie in Grenzgebieten* (pp. 45–63). Würzburg: Ergon.

Hirsch, M. (2008). *Liebe auf Abwegen. Spielarten der Liebe im Film psychoanalytisch betrachtet*. Gießen: Psychosozial.

Hofmann, L., & Roesler, C. (2010). Der Archetyp des verwundeten Heilers. *Transpersonale Psychologie und Psychotherapie, 16*(1), 75–90.

Hogenson, G. B. (2001). The Baldwin Effect: A neglected influence on C. G. Jung's evolutionary thinking. *Journal of Analytical Psychology, 46* (4), 591–611.

Hogenson, G. B. (2004). Archetypes: Emergence and the psyche's deep structure. In J. Cambray & L. Carter (Eds.). *Analytical psychology: Contemporary perspectives in Jungian psychology* (pp. 32–55). New York: Brunner-Routledge.

Huston, H. (1992). *Direct and indirect tests of archetypal memory*. [Unpublished master's thesis]. Texas A&M University. College Station.

Huston, H. L., Rosen, D. H., & Smith, S. M. (1999). Evolutionary memory. In D. H. Rosen & M. C. Luebbert (Eds.). *Evolution of the psyche* (pp. 139–149). Westport: Praeger.

Jacobi, J. (1965). *Der Weg der Individuation*. Zürich: Rascher.

Jacobi, J. (1986). *Die Psychologie von C. G. Jung: Eine Einführung in das Gesamtwerk*. Frankfurt/M.: Fischer.

Jacoby, M. (1993). *Übertragung und Beziehung in der Jungschen Praxis*. Düsseldorf: Walter.

Johnson, M. H., & Morton, J. (1991). *Biology and cognitive development: The case of face recognition*. Oxford: Blackwell.

Jones, R. (2007). *Jung, psychology, postmodernity*. Hove: Routledge.

Jung, C. G. (1919). Instinct and the unconscious. *The British Journal of Psychology, 10*(1), 15–23.

Jung, C. G. (1989–2008). *Collected Works*, 20 vol. London: Routledge (quoted as CW #Vol.).

Jung, C. G., Franz, M.-L. v., Henderson, J. L., Jacobi, J., & Jaffé, A. (1968). *Man and his symbols*. New York: Dell Publishing.

Jung, E. (1967). *Anima und Animus*. Zürich: Rascher.

Jungaberle, H., Verres, R., & Dubois, F. (Eds.) (2006). *Rituale erneuern*. Gießen: Psychosozial.

Kandel, E. R. (2006). *In search of memory. The emergence of a new science of mind*. New York: W. W. Norton.

Kast, V. (1984). *Paare. Beziehungsfantasien oder wie Götter sich in Menschen spiegeln*. Stuttgart: Kreuz.

Kast V. (1990). *Die Dynamik der Symbole. Grundlagen der Jungschen Psychotherapie*. Olten: Walter.

Kast, V. (1999). *Der Schatten in uns. Die subversive Lebenskraft*. Zürich, Düsseldorf: Walter.

Kern, H. (1999). *Labyrinthe*. München: Prestel.

Kirsch, T. (2000). *The Jungians. A comparative and historical perspective*. Abingdon: Routledge.

Klein, M. (1957). *New directions in psycho-analysis : The significance of infant conflict in the pattern of adult behavior*. New York: Basic Books.

Kluckhohn, C. (1960). Recurrent themes in myth and mythmaking. In H. A. Murray (Ed.). *Myth and mythmaking* (pp. 46–60). New York: Braziler.

Knox, J. (2001). Memories, fantasies, archetypes: An exploration of some connections between cognitive science and analytical psychology. *Journal of Analytical Psychology, 46*(4), 613–635.

Knox, J. (2003). *Archetype, attachment, analysis. Jungian psychology and the emergent mind*. Hove: Brunner-Routledge.

Knox, J. (2004). From archetypes to reflective function. *Journal of Analytical Psychology, 49*, 1–19.

Knox, J. (2009). Mirror neurons and embodied simulation in the development of archetypes and self-agency. *Journal of Analytical Psychology, 54*, 307–323.

Krause, R. (2010). Affects, regulation of relationship, transference and countertransference. *International Forum of Psychoanalysis, 8*(2), 103–114. https://doi.org/10.1080/080370699436429

Kut, E., Schaffner, N., Wittwer, A., Candia, V., Brockmann, M., Storck, C., & Folkers, G. (2007). Changes in self-perceived role identity modulate pain perception. *Pain, 131*, 191–201.

Laszig, P. (2013). Blade Runner, Matrix *und* Avatare. *Psychoanalytische Betrachtungen virtueller Wesen und Welten im Film*. Berlin: Springer.

Lawrence, J. S., & Jewett, R. (2002). *The myth of the American superhero*. Grand Rapids: W. B. Eerdmans.

Lesmeister, R. (Hrsg.) (2002). *Ideengeschichtliche Ursprünge und Perspektiven der Psychologie von C. G. Jung.* Basel: Karger.

Levi-Strauss, C. (1976). *Structural anthropology.* New York: Basic Books.

Lichtenberg, J. (1983). Psychoanalysis and infant research. Hillsdale: Analytic Press.

Lorenzer, A. (1986). Tiefenhermeneutische Kulturanalyse. In H.-D. König (Hrsg.). *Kultur-Analysen* (pp. 88–123). Frankfurt/M.: Suhrkamp.

Maloney, A. (1999). Preference ratings of images representing archetypal themes: an empirical study of the concept of archetypes. *Journal of Analytical Psychology, 44,* 101–116.

Marcus, G. (2004). *The birth of the mind: How a tiny number of genes creates the complexities of human thought.* New York: Basic Books.

Masters, R. E. L., & Houston, J. (1966). *The variety of psychedelic experience.* New York: Dell.

Meaney, M. J. (2010). Epigenetics and the biological definition of gene x environment interactions. *Child Development, 81,* 41–79.

Merchant, J. (2006). The developmental/emergent model of archetype, its implications and its application to shamanism. *Journal of Analytical Psychology, 51,* 125–144.

Merchant J. (2009). Reappraisal of classical archetype theory. *Journal of Analytical Psychology, 54,* 339–358.

Merchant, J. (2012). *Shamans and analysts. New insights on the wounded healer.* London: Routledge.

Metzger, W. (1954). *Psychologie. Die Entwicklung ihrer Grundannahmen seit der Einführung des Experiments.* Darmstadt: Steinkopff.

Moore, R., & Gillette, D. (1991). *King, warrior, magician, lover.* New York, San Francisco: Harper Collins, Harper One.

Moore, T. (1996). *The re-enchantment of everyday life.* New York: HarperCollins.

Müller, L., & Müller, A. (Hrsg.) (2003). *Wörterbuch der analytischen Psychologie.* Düsseldorf: Walter.

Neumann, E. (1968). *Ursprungsgeschichte des Bewusstseins.* München: Kindler.

Neumann, E. (1974). *Die große Mutter. Eine Phänomenologie der weiblichen Gestaltungen des Unbewussten.* Zürich: Walter.

Obrist, W. (1990). *Archetypen: Natur- und Kulturwissenschaften bestätigen C. G. Jung.* Olten: Walter.

Österreicher-Mollwo, M. (1990). *Herder Lexikon Symbole.* Freiburg: Herder.

Oxidine, S. A. (2001). *Healing into death: How does individuation as described by C. G. Jung unfold in adults age 65 and over who perceive themselves to be nearing death?* [Doctoral dissertation]. California Institute of Integral Studies. San Francisco.

Papadopoulos, R. (1996). Archetypal family therapy. In L. S. Dodson & T. L. Gibson (Eds.). *Psyche and family. Jungian applications to family therapy* (pp. 81–103). Wilmette, IL: Chiron.

Pearson, C. S., & Marr, H. K. (2003). *PMAI Manual: A guide to interpreting the Pearson-Marr Archetype Indicator instrument.* Gainesville, FL: CAPT.

Pearson, C. S., & Marr, H. K. (2007). *What story are you living? A workbook and guide to interpreting results from the PMAI.* Gainesville, FL: CAPT.

Pederson-Schaefer, K. (2002). *Women's midlife transition experiences: Archetypes and the influence of Western cultural values.* [Doctoral dissertation]. The Wright Institute. Berkeley.

Petzold, H. G., Orth, I., & Sieper, J. (2014). *Mythen, Macht und Psychotherapie.* Bielefeld: Aisthesis.

Pietikainen, P. (1998). Archetypes as symbolic forms. *Journal of Analytical Psychology, 43*(3), 325–343.

Prendergast, L. (2005). *Transformation to meaning in late midlife men.* [Doctoral dissertation]. Fielding Graduate Institute. Santa Barbara.

Propp, V. (1975). *Morphologie des Märchens.* Frankfurt/M.: Suhrkamp.

Rauwald, M. (2013). *Vererbte Wunden. Transgenerationelle Weitergabe traumatischer Erfahrungen.* Weinheim: Beltz.

Riedel, I. (1985a). *Formen: Kreis, Kreuz, Dreieck, Quadrat, Spirale.* Stuttgart: Kreuz.

Riedel, I. (1985b). *Farben in Religion, Gesellschaft, Kunst und Psychotherapie.* Stuttgart: Kreuz.

Riedel, I. (1989). *Die weise Frau in uralt-neuen Erfahrungen.* Olten, Freiburg: Walter.

Rittner, S. (2006). Trance und Ritual in Psychotherapie und Forschung. In H. Jungaberle, R. Verres, & F. DuBois (Hrsg.). *Rituale erneuern. Ritualdynamik und Grenzerfahrung aus interdisziplinärer Perspektive* (pp. 165–192). Gießen: Psychosozial.

Rizzolati, G., & Craighero, L. (2004). The mirror-neuron system. *Annual Review of Neuroscience, 27,* 169–192.

Roesler, C. (2005). Narrative Biographieforschung und archetypische Geschichtenmuster. In I. Meier, G. Mattanza, & M. Schlegel (Hrsg.).

Seele und Forschung. Ein Brückenschlag in der Psychotherapie (pp. 214–233). Basel: Karger.

Roesler, C. (2006). A narratological methodology for identifying archetypal story patterns in autobiographical narratives. *The Journal of Analytical Psychology, 51*(4), pp. 574–596.

Roesler, C. (2010). *Analytische Psychologie heute. Der aktuelle Forschungsstand zur Psychologie C. G. Jungs.* Basel, Freiburg: Karger.

Roesler, C. (2011). The meaning of conflict in couples. A Jungian approach to couples therapy. In S. Wirth, I. Meier, & J. Hill (Eds.). *Trust and betrayal: Dawnings of consciousness* (pp. 117–130). New Orleans: Spring.

Roesler, C. (2012a). A revision of Jung's theory of archetypes in the light of contemporary research: neurosciences, genetics and cultural theory – a reformulation. In P. Bennett (Ed.). *Facing multiplicity: Psyche, nature, culture* (pp. 961–981). Proceedings of the XVIIIth Congress of the International Association for Analytical Psychology, Montreal 2010 (28–37). Einsiedeln: Daimon.

Roesler, C. (2012b). Are archetypes transmitted more by culture than biology? Questions arising from conceptualizations of the archetype. *Journal of Analytical Psychology, 57*, 224–247.

Roesler, C. (2013). Das gemeinsame Unbewußte – Unbewußte Austausch- und Synchronisierungsprozesse in der Psychotherapie und in nahen Beziehungen. *Analytische Psychologie, 44*(4), 464–483.

Roesler, C. (2014). A research frame for investigating the appearance of synchronistic events in psychotherapy. In H. Atmanspacher & C. Fuchs (Eds.). *The Pauli-Jung dialogue and Its Impact Today* (pp. 241–254). Exeter: Imprint Academic.

Roesler, C., & Giebeler, D. (2015). Synchronizität: sinnvolle Koinzidenzen. In G. Mayer, M. Schetsche, I. Schmied-Knittel, & D. Vaitl (Hrsg.). *An den Grenzen der Erkenntnis. Handbuch der wissenschaftlichen Anomalistik* (pp. 243–255). Stuttgart: Schattauer.

Roesler, C., & van Uffelen, B. (2018). Complexes and the unconscious: From the Association Experiment to recent fMRI studies. In C. Roesler (Ed.). *Research in analytical psychology* (pp. 85–97). London: Routledge.

Rohr, R. (1996). *The wild man's journey.* Cincinnati: St Anthony Messenger Press.

Rosen, D. H., Smith, S. M., Huston, H. L., & Gonzalez, G. (1991). Empirical study of associations between symbols and their meaning: Evidence of collective unconscious (archetypal) memory. *Journal of Analytical Psychology, 36*, 211–228.

Rudolf, G. (2000). *Psychotherapeutische Medizin und Psychosomatik.* Stuttgart: Thieme.

Samuels, A. (1986). *Jung and the post-Jungians.* Abingdon: Routledge.

Samuels, A., Shorter, B., & Plaut, F. (1986). *A critical dictionary of Jungian analysis.* Abingdon: Routledge.

Sanford, J. A. (1991). *Unsere unsichtbaren Partner.* Interlaken: Ansata.

Saunders, P., & Skar, P. (2001). Archetypes, complexes and self-organisation. *Journal of Analytical Psychology, 46*(2), 305–323.

Scharff, D. E., & Scharff, J. S. (2014). *Das interpersonelle Unbewusste. Perspektiven einer beziehungsorientierten Psychoanalyse.* Gießen: Psychosozial.

Schellenbaum, P. (1994). *Aggression zwischen Liebenden.* Hamburg: Hoffmann und Campe.

Schellenbaum, P. (1995). *Nimm deine Couch und geh: Heilung mit Spontanritualen.* München: dtv.

Schick, A. (2015). *Selbsterfahrung Mann : therapeutische Zugangswege zur Männerseele.* Berlin, Heidelberg: Springer.

Schwartz-Salant, N. (1995). On the interactive field as the analytic object. In M. Stein (Ed.). *The interactive field in analysis* (pp. 38–57). Wilmette, IL: Chiron.

Schwartz-Salant, N. (1998). *The mystery of human relationship.* London: Routledge.

Seifert, T. (1975). Analytische Psychologie im Rahmen empirischer Forschung. *Analytische Psychologie, 6*(22), 507–523.

Seiter, C. (2003): Ist ein direkter Transfer von ereignisbezogenen Potentialen (ERPs) im EEG nachzuweisen? In W. Belschner, L. Hofmann, & H. Walach (Hrsg.). *Auf dem Weg zu einer Psychologue des Bewusstseins* (pp. 47–58). Oldenburg: BIS.

Seligman, M. E., & Hager, J. L. (1972). *Biological boundaries of learning.* Appleton, WI: Century-Crofts.

Shamdasani, S. (2003). *Jung and the making of modern psychology: The dream of a science.* Cambridge: Cambridge University Press.

Shelburne, W. A. (1988). *Mythos and logos in the thought of Carl Jung. The theory of the collective unconscious in scientific perspective.* Albany: State University of New York Press.

Singer, T., & Kimbles, J. (2004). Emerging theory of cultural complexes. In J. Cambray & L. Carter (Eds.). *Analytical psychology: Contemporary perspectives in Jungian psychology* (pp. 176–203). New York: Brunner-Routledge.

Skar, P. (2004). Chaos and self-organization: Emergent patterns at critical life transitions. *Journal of Analytical Psychology*, 49(2), 245–264.

Sotirova-Kohli, M., Roesler, C., Opwis, K., Smith, S., Rosen, D., & Djonov, V. (2013). Symbol/Meaning paired-associate recall: An 'archetypal memory' advantage? *Behavioural Science, 3*(4), 541–561.

Sotirova-Kohli, M., Rosen, D. H., Smith, S. M., Henderson, P., & Taki-Reece, S. (2011). Empirical study of kanji as archetypal images: Understanding the collective unconscious as part of the Japanese language. *Journal of Analytical Psychology, 56*, 109–132.

Spitz, R. (1965). *Vom Säugling zum Kleinkind.* Stuttgart: Klett-Cotta.

Stadler, M., & Kruse, P. (1990). The self-organisation perspective in cognition research: Historical remarks and new experimental approaches. In H. Haken & M. Stadler (Eds.). *Synergetics of cognition* (pp. 32–53). Berlin: Springer.

Stadler, P. (1997). Archetyp, Geschichte, Traum: Ihre Beziehung zu Prozessen psychischer Abwehr. *Analytische Psychologie, 28*, 273–282.

Staufenberg, A. (2011). *Zur Psychoanalyse der ADHS: Manual und Katamnese.* Frankfurt/M.: Brandes & Apsel.

Steffen, U. (1989). *Drachenkampf – der Mythos vom Bösen.* Stuttgart: Kreuz.

Stein, M. (Ed.) (1995). *The interactive field in analysis.* Wilmette: Chiron.

Stephens, G. J., Silbert, L. J., & Hasson, U. (2010). Speaker–listener neural coupling underlies successful communication. Proceedings of the National Academy of Sciences of the United States of America Early Edition, www.pnas.org/cgi/doi/10.1073/pnas.1008662107

Stern, D. (1985). *The interpersonal world of the infant : A view from psychoanalysis and developmental psychology.* New York: Basic Books.

Stevens, A. (1983). *Archetype: A natural history of the self.* New York: William Morrow.

Stevens, A. (2003). *Archetype revisited: An updated natural history of the Self.* Toronto: Inner City Books.

Stevens, A., & Price, J. (1996). *Evolutionary psychiatry.* London: Routledge.

Strauß, B., Buchheim, A., & Kächele, H. (Hrsg.) (2002). *Klinische Bindungsforschung.* Stuttgart: Schattauer.

Teichert, W. (1986). *Gärten – paradiesische Kulturen.* Stuttgart: Kreuz.

Tinbergen, N. (1978). *Laborversuche und Schriften zur Ethologie.* München: Piper.

Tresan, D. I. (1996). Jungian metapsychology and neurobiological theory. *Journal of Analytical Psychology, 41,* 399–436.

Tronick, E. (1998). *Interventions that effect change in psychotherapy: A model based on infant research.* East Lansing: World Association on Infant Mental Health.

Turnbull, O., & Solms, M. (2005). Gedächtnis und Phantasie. In V. Green (Hrsg.). *Emotionale Entwicklung in Psychoanalyse, Bindungstheorie und Neurowissenschaften* (pp. 69–114). Frankfurt/ M.: Brandes & Apsel.

Twillman, N. M. (2000). Archetypes and weight loss. *The NF Journal, 7*(5), 10–12.

Vezzoli C. (2009). Introduction to papers from the conference on 'Neuroscience and Analytical Psychology: Archetypes, Intentionality, Action and Symbols'. *Journal of Analytical Psychology, 54,* 303–305.

Vogler, C. (1997). *Die Odyssee des Drehbuchschreibers. Über die mythologischen Grundmuster des amerikanischen Erfolgskinos.* Frankfurt/M.: Zweitausendeins.

von Beit, H. (1952–57). *Symbolik des Märchens.* Bern: Francke.

von Franz, M.-L. (1986). *Psychologische Märcheninterpretation.* München: Kösel.

von Franz, M.-L. (1991). *Der Schatten und das Böse im Märchen.* München: Knaur.

von Franz, M.-L. (1992). *Der ewige Jüngling.* München: Kösel.

von Franz, M.-L. (1997). *Das Weibliche im Märchen.* Leinfelden-Echterdingen: Bonz.

von Gontard, A. (2007). *Theorie und Praxis der Sandspieltherapie.* Stuttgart: Kohlhammer.

Walden, T. (2015). *Hollywoodpädagogik.* München: Kopaed.

Wehr, G. (1998). *Heilige Hochzeit – Symbol und Erfahrung menschlicher Reifung.* München: Diederichs.

Weiss, E. R. (Hrsg.) (1922). *Homers Odyssee*; Griechisch-Deutsch, in der Übersetzung von Johann Heinrich Voss. Berlin, Leipzig: Tempel.

Wilson, E. O. (2012). *The social conquest of earth.* New York: Liveright.

Witzel, M. (2012). *The origins of the world's mythologies.* Oxford: Oxford University Press.

Zerling, C., & Bauer, W. (2003). *Lexikon der Tiersymbolik.* München: Kösel.

Zoja, L. (Ed.) (2002). *Jungian reflections on September 11. A global nightmare.* Einsiedeln: Daimon.

Zoja, L. (2009). *Violence in history, culture and the psyche.* New Orleans: Spring.

Index

For Product Safety Concerns and Information please contact our EU
representative GPSR@taylorandfrancis.com
Taylor & Francis Verlag GmbH, Kaufingerstraße 24, 80331 München, Germany